AF705971

Property and Trust Law in Spain

Property and Trust Law in Spain

Third Edition

Rafael Sánchez Aristi
Nieves Moralejo Imbernón

This bock was originally published as a monograph in the International Encyclopaedia of Laws/Property and Trust Law.

Founding Editor: Roger Blanpain
General Editor: Frank Hendrickx
Volume Editors: Alain Verbeke & Vincent Sagaert

Wolters Kluwer

Published by:
Kluwer Law International B.V.
PO Box 316
2400 AH Alphen aan den Rijn
The Netherlands
E-mail: international-sales@wolterskluwer.com
Website: lrus.wolterskluwer.com

Sold and distributed in North, Central and South America by:
Wolters Kluwer Legal & Regulatory U.S.
7201 McKinney Circle
Frederick, MD 21704
United States of America
Email: customer.service@wolterskluwer.com

Sold and distributed in all other countries by:
Air Business Subscriptions
Rockwood House
Haywards Heath
West Sussex
RH16 3DH
United Kingdom
Email: international-customerservice@wolterskluwer.com

ISBN 978-94-035-1344-7

e-Book: ISBN 978-94-035-1373-7
web-PDF: ISBN 978-94-035-1411-6

This title is available on www.kluwerlawonline.com

The Authors

Prof. Dr Rafael Sánchez Aristi (14 May 1969) is chair professor on Civil Law of the Faculty of Social and Juridical Sciences at the Rey Juan Carlos University in Madrid, Spain (2018). In 2015, he joined the firm Uría Menéndez as a consultant. He received his doctorate (PhD) in Law, with honours, from the Autónoma University in Madrid, with a thesis on Copyright in Musical Works (1998), made under the direction of Prof. Dr Rodrigo Bercovitz Rodríguez-Cano. He was granted the First 'Sancho Rebullida' Award by the Law School of the Navarre University in Pamplona for the best thesis on Civil Law defended in Spain during the academic year 1997–1998. He has written a book, corresponding to his thesis, (Granada, Comares, two editions: 1999 and 2005), a second one on successory agreements (Granada, Comares, 2003) and another one on the issue of peer-to-peer file-sharing (Madrid, Instituto de Derecho de Autor, 2007). He has enjoyed a research scholarship within a Research Personnel Training Programme implemented by the Autonomous Community of Madrid (1993–1997) and member of several research projects on various subjects concerning intellectual property financed by the Ministry of Education. He has been a visiting researcher at the Max Planck Institute for Patent, Copyright, and Competition Law in Munich (Germany) and at King's College in London (United Kingdom). For twenty years, he has been the first coordinator and later vice director, as well as regular contributor of the review *pe. i. revista de propiedad intelectual*, the sole four-monthly publication in Spanish devoted monographically to the study of intellectual property. He has participated in several collective works, such as *A Comment on the Law on Standard-Form Contracts* (Pamplona, Aranzadi, 1999), *A Comment on the Civil Code* (Pamplona, Aranzadi, three editions: 2001, 2006, 2009, 2013), *A Comment on the Bankruptcy Law* (Tecnos, Madrid, 2004), *A Comment on the Intellectual Property Law* (Tecnos, Madrid, 2007), *A Treatise on Contracts Law* (Tirant lo Blanch, Valencia, 2009, 2013), and *A Handbook on Intellectual Property* (Valencia, Tirant lo Blanch, five editions: 2001, 2003, 2006, 2009, 2012, 2015), all of them edited by Prof. Dr R. Bercovitz. Among other studies, his article on Purchase by Law of Property and Other Real Rights in Goods (*Aranzadi Civil*, No. 19 (February 2001), 13) is particularly noteworthy.

In 2015, his work *La propiedad trenzada: el juego de lo material y lo inmaterial en las obras de arte* ('The Braided Property: The Play of the Material and the Immaterial in the Works of Art') has been awarded the First Prize 'Rodrigo Uría Meruéndano de Derecho del Arte' (2015).

He has taken part as rapporteur in many courses and seminars, lecturing about several matters, mainly related to intellectual property rights, under invitation of entities and organizations such as the World Intellectual Property Organization, the European Institute for Public Administration, the Spanish Group of the *Association Littéraire et Artistique Internationale*, the International University 'Menéndez Pelayo', the Cervantes Institute, the *Sociedad General de Autores y Editores*, the Autónoma University of Madrid, the University of Alicante, the University of Castilla-La Mancha and the Spanish Association of Writers, among others.

As a teacher, he has taught throughout a period of twenty years all subjects of traditional divisions of Civil Law (General Part, Persons, Obligations and Contracts, Property and Trust Law, Family and Successions Law). For several years he has been in charge of teaching the special subjects on Intellectual Property at the Faculty of Social and Juridical Sciences of the Rey Juan Carlos University in Madrid. Having been the Secretary (2007–2015), he is currently the President of the Spanish Group of the *Association Littéraire et Artistique Internationale.*

He has been lawyer-director of studies and reports in the Consejo General del Poder Judicial (General Council for the Judiciary) (2009–2014), and he served as a deputy judge in the Audiencia Provincial de Guadalajara (Provincial Court of Guadalajara) (2007–2009).

Prof. Dr Nieves Moralejo Imbernón (10 July 1970) is a tenured lecturer on Civil Law at the Faculty of Law of the Autónoma University in Madrid (Spain). She received her doctorate (PhD) in Law, with honours, by the Autónoma University in Madrid, with a thesis on the administration of goods belonging to the marriage partnership, made under the direction of Prof. Dr R. Bercovitz. She has written a book, corresponding to her thesis, titled *Actos de administración de bienes gananciales realizados por el cónyuge titular o poseedor* (Granada, Comares, 1998), another one on the lease of an enterprise as a whole, titled *El arrendamiento de empresa* (Pamplona, Aranzadi, 2004), and a third one, titled *The Mortgage Contract* (Cizur Menor, Aranzadi Thomson Reuters, 2010). Along with Professor Sánchez Aristi and a third co-author, she has published a book about the ECJ case law on intellectual property rights, titled *La Jurisprudencia del Tribunal de Justicia de la Unión Europea en materia de propiedad intelectual* (Madrid, Instituto de Derecho de Autor, 2017).

She has taught all subjects into which the Civil Law is traditionally divided, both at the Faculty of Law of the Autónoma University in Madrid and at the Faculty of Law of the University in Vigo (Spain). She has enjoyed a research scholarship within a Research Personnel Training Programme implemented by the Ministry of Education (1994–1998), another two within a Research Programme for Professors Seniors (September–December 2009, February–April 2015) at Columbia University (New York) and at the Max Planck Institute for Innovation and

Competition of Munich (Germany), implemented as well by the Ministry of Education and finally one within a Research Programme for Professors Seniors (September–December 2012) at Catholic University (Washington DC) implemented by Bankia. More recently, she has enjoyed a research scholarship within the Mobility Programme for Professors of the Universities that belong to Red Yerum at Tor Vergata University (Italy), implemented by the International Relations Vice rectorate of the Autónoma University of Madrid (November 2017–February 2018).

Her main contributions have been made in the field of marriage partnership. Her articles on the seizure of goods belonging to the marriage partnership (*Aranzadi Civil*, No. 19 (February 1999), 15) and on the private rules about the family home (*El patrimonio familiar, profesional y empresarial. Sus protocolos*. Barcelona, Bosch, 2005) stand out in particular. Furthermore, she has participated in several collective works such as a series on practical cases in Civil Law (Madrid, Universidad Autónoma de Madrid, 1997–1999), a series on Handbooks on Civil Law (Madrid, Bercal. 2005, 2007, 2008), a Comment on the Law on Standard-Form Contracts (Pamplona, Aranzadi, 1999), a Comment on the Civil Code (Pamplona, Aranzadi, 2001, 2004, 2009, 2013), a Comment on the Bankruptcy Law (Madrid, Tecnos, 2004), a Comment on the Intellectual Property Law (Cizur Menor, Aranzadi, 2007), a Comment on the Consumers Law (Cizur Menor, Aranzadi, 2009, 2014), a Treatise on Contracts Law (Valencia, Tirant lo Blanch 2009, 2013), another Comment on the Civil Code (Valencia, Tirant lo Blanch, 2013) and a Comment on the Berne Convention (Madrid, Tecnos, 2013) all of them edited by Prof. Dr R. Bercovitz. In the field of Intellectual Property, she has published an article on Intellectual Property Spanish Register that has been published in *pe. i. Revista de Propiedad Intelectual* (No. 26, 2007) and another one on Intellectual Property and Marriage (Estudios de Propiedad Intelectual, 2016).

Since 2010, she is the Secretary of the above-mentioned review *pe.i. Revista de propiedad intelectual*.

The Authors

Acknowledgements

The authors wish to state their deep feelings of gratitude and admiration to Prof. Dr D. Rodrigo Bercovitz Rodríguez-Cano, who has never failed to give them his support and encouragement. They also want to express their pride in belonging to the research team that Prof. Dr R. Bercovitz, as Professor in Civil Law at the Faculty of Law of the Autonóma University in Madrid (Spain), has formed for the last thirty years. This monograph must be seen as one of the fruits produced by this team.

The authors also wish to thank María A. Álvarez San José for her inestimable help with the translation of this book from Spanish into English.

Acknowledgements

Table of Contents

Table of Contents

List of Abbreviations

Although we have translated into English the names to which the abbreviations refer, we have maintained the abbreviations that are normally used by Spanish scholars and courts. Regarding laws, the date of the original approval is given, although in the major part of the cases they have been subjected to one or more reforms.

CC	Civil Code (24 July 1889)
CC AA	Autonomous Communities
Ccom	Commercial Code (22 August 1885)
CE	Spanish Constitution (27 December 1978)
ECJ	European Court of Justice
GDP	Gross Domestic Product
LAR	Law on Rural Leases (Law 49/2003, 26 November 2003)
LAU	Law on Urban Leases (Law 29/1994, 24 November 1994)
LCAT	Law on Contracts of Exploitation in Shifts of Buildings for Use by Tourism (Law 4/2012, 6 July 2012)
LEC	Law on Civil Procedures (Law 1/2000, 7 January 2000)
LEF	Law on Mandatory Expropriation (16 December 1954)
LH	Law on Land Registry (8 February 1946)
LHMPDP	Law on Movable Mortgage and Pledge without Transfer of Possession (16 December 1954)
LM	Law on Trademarks (Law 17/2001, 7 December 2001)
LP	Law on Patents (Law 24/2015, 24 July 2015)
LPAP	Law on Public Administration Patrimony (Law 33/2003, 3 November 2003)
LPH	Law on Joint Ownership of Blocks of Flats (Law 49/1960, 21 July 1960)
LPJDI	Law on Juridical Protection of Industrial Design (Law 20/2003, 7 July)
LRDA	Law on Agrarian Reform and Development (Law 118/1973, 12 January 1973)
LSC	Law on Companies (Royal Legislative Decree 1/2010, 2 July 2010)

List of Abbreviations

LVPBM	Law on Sale on Credit of Movable Goods (Law 28/1998, 13 July 1998)
OECD	Organisation for Economic Co-operation and Development
RH	Regulation on Land Registry (Decree 14 February 1947)
RJA	Aranzadi Compilation of Jurisprudence
SSTS	Sentences of the Supreme Court
STC	Sentence of the Constitutional Court
STS	Sentence of the Supreme Court
TC	Constitutional Court
TRLMV	Law on the Securities Market (Legislative Decree 4/2015, 23 October 2015)
TRLS	Law on Land (Legislative Decree 7/2015, 30 October 2015)
TS	Supreme Court

General Introduction

Chapter 1. General Background of the Country

§1. Geography

1. Spain is a country located in the extreme southwest part of Europe. With its 500,000 km^2 it is the fourth European country in area, and with its 46.4 million inhabitants (2015), it is the seventh most populated one. Nevertheless, the average population density is relatively low (92 people per km^2), with large variations among regions. Together with its neighbour Portugal, Spain occupies the territory of the Iberian Peninsula.

Apart from the continental area, two archipelagos also make up Spain's land mass: the Balearic Islands (located in the Mediterranean Sea) and the Canary Islands (located in the Atlantic Ocean). Two small towns located on the north coast of Morocco (Ceuta and Melilla) also belong to Spain. Consequently, Spain has land frontiers not only with Portugal and Morocco but also with France. The border between France and Spain consists of a well-known chain of mountains: the Pyrenees. In fact, Spain also has a land frontier with the Principality of Andorra, a small country located in the Eastern Pyrenees and completely bordered by Spain and France. It must also be mentioned that the small self-governing British overseas territory of Gibraltar, which is located at the southern end of the Iberian Peninsula, shares a land border with Spain to its north. Its area covers less than 7 km^2.

The capital city of Spain is Madrid, which is situated in the middle of the territory. Madrid's metropolitan area has a population of approximately 6.2 million inhabitants (2016). Other main cities and metropolitan areas in the country are Barcelona (5.1 million), Valencia (1.5 million), Seville (1.3 million), and Malaga (1 million).

2. From a topographic point of view, Spain has an uneven terrain. In fact, after Switzerland, it has the most-varied terrain of all European countries, with an average height of more than 600 m. It has a vast central plateau and five big cordilleras distributed from north to south (Pyrenees, Cantabrian, Iberian, Central, and *Bética*), not including other minor chains of mountains. Some of its peaks rise to more than 3,000 m in height. These characteristics have traditionally made its internal communications difficult and have also caused some regions to be isolated. Another reason for that is that, in contrast with other countries, Spain has few navigable rivers. However, due to its 3,500-km-long coastline, Spain does have suitable conditions for sea navigation. For many centuries, Spain has been a country open to fishing, sea transport, and (historically) marine military invasions and expansions.

3. Spain is, for the most part, a Mediterranean-climate country, although in the northern part, from Galicia to the Pyrenees, there is an oceanic climate, very similar to the British climate (annual precipitations of more than 1,000 mm). An extreme aridity predominates in southeastern regions, with an almost total absence of precipitation (less than 300 mm per annum). The annual average temperatures vary appreciably among regions. In the northland and inland, temperatures range from 0°C to 6°C in winter and from 18°C to 24°C in summer. In coastal zones, especially those bathed by the Mediterranean Sea, temperatures are about 6°C–12°C in winter and 24°C–30°C in summer. The Canary Islands have an annual average temperature of more than 20°C.

4. In Spain, vegetable species characteristic of the Mediterranean wood (Holm oaks, cork oaks and several species of bush) prevail. Dry farming (vine, olive) is more extensive than irrigation farming. Spain is a great producer of wine and the highest producer of olive oil in the world. It also produces a great number of fruits and vegetables, which are cultivated mainly in the areas of Valencia and Murcia. Regarding cattle raising, according to data from 2005, the more prevalent are the porcine and the ovine (25 and 23 million heads, respectively), against the bovine (6.5 million heads) and the goatish (3 million heads). Spain is, however, one of Europe's largest producers and consumers of maritime fishing.

5. Spain ranks among the ten largest mineral-producing countries in the world, energy materials (coal, petroleum, gas and uranium) excluded. It does maintain, however, a certain level of coal extraction activity in several provinces to the north, but Spanish resources of gas and petroleum are almost non-existent. There are relatively important beds of both metallic (steel, copper, pyrites, lead, tin, mercury and wolfram) and non-metallic (quartz, potassium or marine salt) minerals. Although the production of metallic minerals is unable to satisfy domestic demand, the existence of non-metallic minerals is marked by surplus and far exceeds the needs of the national market.

Although some nuclear power stations of great potency continue operations, only 20% of the Spanish energy production came from this source in 2008. In the same year, conventional sectors such as fossil fuels and hydraulic power reached 56% of the total generation. But Spain is making a strong bet on renewable energy sources, which is shown by the fact that in 2008, the total electricity produced with renewable energy sources satisfied 24% of the demand, with approximately half of that amount coming from wind power. In fact, Spain is the second largest producer of wind power in Europe, after Germany, and the fourth in the world, behind China, the United States (US) and Germany (World Wind Energy Report, 2011), with an installed capacity of 21,288 MW (2012). Due to this factor, Spain has overcome its traditional deficit of electric energy production. Nevertheless, as is the case with other countries, the systems of solar energy exploitation are not yet fully developed, in spite of the enormous potential that this energy has in a country with as many sun hours as Spain (more than 2,500 hours of sun every year in most parts of its territory).

6. Its mild and sunny weather, together with other factors, has made Spain a top tourist destination and has allowed tourism to become one of the main industries in the country. It was the second country in both numbers of international tourist arrivals (81.8 million visitors) and international tourism receipts (USD 68 billion) for 2017 (according to World Tourism Organization's statistics). Among the factors that contribute to Spain being one of the most-visited countries, the most notable are the beauty and good state of maintenance of many natural spaces, both beaches and mountain areas (some of which have been appointed as areas of special protection due to their high ecologic value), its enormous monumental and cultural patrimony, its cuisine, its popular festivities, and the hospitable character of the Spanish people.

7. The number of immigrants registered to live in Spain permanently has changed considerably since 2000, when 900,000 were officially counted (only 2.2% of the total population). For the year 2012, the foreign population has grown to 5.7 million people (12.1% of the total population): 1.5 million of European origin, 1.5 million from Central and South America, and another 800,000 from Africa, mainly from Morocco. Currently, Spain has the second highest immigration rates within the European Union (EU; Spain was Europe's largest absorber of migrants from 2002 to 2007) and the second highest absolute net migration in the world, after the US. These immigration figures are probably related to the recent increase in the fertility rate, which has increased from 1.29 births per woman for the period 2000–2005 to 1.41 births per woman for the period 2005–2010. Life expectancy at birth is one of the highest both in Europe and in the world: 77.7 years for men and 84.2 years for women (according to United Nations data for the period 2005–2010).

8. The Spanish Gross Domestic Product (GDP) reached more than USD 1.3 billion in 2017 (according to the International Monetary Fund data at current market prices and current exchange rates), which places Spain in the fourteenth position in the world. However, its GDP per capita reached USD 32,700 in 2012 (according to Organisation for Economic Co-operation and Development (OECD) data at purchasing power parity levels), which means the twentieth position within OECD countries. The rate of economic growth in Spain was higher than the OECD average until the beginning of the current global economic crisis (3.5% for the period 1998–2008), but then it passed to negative or neutral figures for a period of five years (-3.6% in 2009, 0.0% in 2010, -1.0% in 2011, -2.6% in 2012 and -1.7% in 2013). In 2014 and 2015 the figures have been positive again: 1.4% and 3.2% respectively, which would indicate, according to main analysts, a recovery from the worst phase of the crisis. As regarding regions, those with higher standards of living are the ones located in the northeast, north of the River Ebro (Catalonia, Navarre, Aragon, La Rioja and Basque Country), together with Madrid and the Balearic Islands.

The global economic crisis of 2008–2013 had particularly severe consequences in Spain. One reason is that between 1998 and 2008, the country's economy had experienced a huge housing bubble, thus a great part of employment was dependent on the building sector. The result was a large unemployment rate (above 25%), which has been reduced later to a rate of 20.8% (December 2015).

§2. Cultural Situation

9. Spain is a nation culturally influenced by the traditions of Western European countries, especially France, Portugal and Italy. As they were, Spain was part of the Roman Empire (Hispania) overtaken in the fourth century by the invasion of Germanic peoples from central Europe. As in those countries, the main official language of the nation (Spanish) is a language derived from Latin, and the predominant religion has always been Catholicism. Nevertheless, Spain has an important historical differential fact with regard to its neighbours: For almost eight centuries (between 711 and 1492) a big part of its territory (practically the whole territory, except for a small area in the north of the Cantabrian cordillera) remained under the political power and the cultural influence of various Muslim peoples, arriving in successive waves from northern Africa and the Middle East. In the tenth century, a Caliphate was even set in the town of Cordoba, which became a fabulous human agglomeration of almost 1 million inhabitants. That singular Muslim influence has left an ineradicable trace on Spaniards' idiosyncrasy.

10. The Muslim presence in Spain was not a hindrance. On the contrary, the Roman Catholic faith grew alongside with enormous vigour, especially in the northern regions where the Islamic influence was weaker. It is not fortuitous that it was in Spain – to be precise, in Santiago de Compostela – where a zealous cult was formed at the sepulchre of one of the twelve apostles of Jesus of Nazareth and to which traditionally a pilgrimage is made from all over Europe following a defined set of routes (Camino de Santiago). This tradition that has survived since the Middle Ages (Santiago de Compostela is, together with Rome and Jerusalem, one of the three pilgrimages most recognized by the Roman Catholic Church) has played an important role in the interchange system between the European and Spanish cultures. Slowly the Roman Catholics spread southward, recovering territories from the Muslims. This effort lasted several centuries and contributed to forming the essence of the Spanish nation. This process of 'Reconquest' concluded in 1492 with the recovery of Granada – the last bastion of Islam in the Iberian Peninsula – by the 'Catholic Monarchs' (Isabella of Castile and Ferdinand of Aragon, whose marriage in 1469 linked not only their personal futures but also the destiny of their two kingdoms).

11. The reign of these two monarchs, at the turn of the fifteenth century, represented the start of the period of the greatest splendour for Spain throughout its history. Apart from finishing the reconquest process and establishing national unity, the Catholic Monarchs encouraged Admiral Colón's project of reaching the East Indies following the western route (i.e., to say, crossing the Atlantic Ocean). Patronized by Queen Isabella of Castile herself, Colón discovered America for Spain in 1492.

Since that moment, the destiny of the American continent has forever been linked to that of Spain, which in the fifteenth century established the first transoceanic empire in history.

The work of the Monarchs Isabella and Ferdinand were continued by their grandson Carlos of Habsburg, whose title as King of Castile and Aragon gave him the control over the American and Mediterranean possessions that those two kingdoms included. His sovereignty also extended to the territories that his paternal grandparents (Mary of Burgundy and Maximilian of Austria) had throughout Europe. Carlos added the title of Emperor of the Sacred Roman-German Empire in 1519, by the decision of the electors of the various princedoms and bishoprics that then constituted current Germany. For the whole of the sixteenth century and until the end of the reign of Carlos' son, Felipe II, Spain was, without doubt, the most powerful nation in the world, economically, culturally and militarily.

It has been said that, given its vast extension throughout the entire world, Spain was then known as the land where 'there was no sunset'.[1] The main mistake that Felipe II committed, and that showed the start of Spain's military decline, was the ineffective invasion of England in 1588 by the 'Armada Invincible' warships.

12. Spain slowly started to decline both politically and economically during the seventeenth century. Its weakness was reflected in the military defeat against the Netherlands, whose independence Spain was forced to recognize as a result of the Westphalia Treaties (1648). When the last Spanish king of the Habsburg, Carlos II, died heirless, a Succession War, both at the internal and international level, began between the partisans of Felipe of Anjou, grandson of the king of France Louis XIV, and the partisans of the archduke Carlos of Austria, son of the Austrian Emperor Joseph I. The conflict ended with a victory for the former and thus with the enthronement of Felipe of Anjou as Felipe V, first Spanish king of the Bourbon dynasty.

However, the outcome of the Succession War, reflected in the Treaty of Utrecht (1713–1714), could not have been worse for the general interests of Spain. On the one hand, Spain was forced to give all its European possessions outside the Peninsula (Naples, Sardinia, Milan, and what is now known as Belgium) in favour of Austria. On the other hand, the Spanish king was obliged to renounce his rights to the French throne and to allow England to maintain Gibraltar and Menorca Island (Balearic), breaking the commercial monopoly with the Spanish colonies in America in England's favour. Finally, at the internal level, the war caused a deep division between the regions that had supported Felipe V (Castile, Navarre and Basque Country) and those that did not (Catalonia, Aragon and Valencia), resulting in the loss of many of their old privileges.

13. During the rest of the seventeenth century, Spain enjoyed relative political and economic stability, and it showed itself open to the Enlightenment's new ideas. The coming of the French Revolution and the events that followed it, including Napoleon being in power, coincided with the presence on the Spanish throne of a

1. All the more so considering that in 1580 Felipe II added the status of King of Portugal, which added the Portuguese possessions in America, Africa and Asia to his father's inheritance.

very weak king who favoured Napoleon marching into Spain with his troops and enthroning his own brother as the new king. These happenings produced, mainly in some towns, a strong popular resistance movement against the French invasion ('Independence War'). In one of them, Cádiz, the first Spanish Constitution (CE) (1812) was approved. This constitution soon became both a symbol of the Spanish people's freedom against the French invaders and, more generally, a symbol of individuals' freedom against the authority exercised by absolute monarchs.

Nevertheless, the (more or less) absolute monarchy continued to control the destiny of the country throughout the nineteenth century, while the Overseas Empire finally crumbled. Only at the end of the century was a minimally stable system of parliamentary monarchy instituted, with two political parties (liberal and conservative) alternatively having control. But during the first decades of the twentieth century, the Spanish parliamentary system deteriorated progressively, the economic penury and the social upheavals causing a whirlwind of disturbances in the country. The defeats suffered in the wars waged by Spain in defence of the last remnants of its Colonial Empire were detrimental.

The situation became so extreme that in 1923 the king (Alfonso XIII) entrusted the government to a military Directorate chaired by General Primo de Rivera. This military dictatorship lasted until 1930, when the fall of the king himself was imminent. In fact, in 1931, after a peaceful electoral process and with strong popular support, Spain became a Republic. The situation remained unchanged for only eight years: After provoking a bloody civil war (1936–1939) and overthrowing the republican regime, General Franco appropriated the government of the nation and began to exercise a dictatorial control that lasted almost four decades (1939–1975). Spain was so battered after its civil war that, although Franco sympathized with the Roma-Berlin Axis and sent some troops as a token of support, the dictator avoided involvement in World War II.

In retrospect, Spain went through a long period of approximately 150 years (1823–1975) of being the victim of its own breakdown as a metropolis, absolutist – if not dictatorial – political governments, the permanent threat of social and regional collapse, an often autarkic state, and a persistent cultural isolation from outside. All of these made Spain a nation greatly reflecting on its own problems and national identity, a feeling that the Spanish people have, over the last thirty-five years, started to leave behind.

14. If analysed in historical perspective, Spain can be considered as one of the largest cultural powers not only in the European sphere but also worldwide. Spanish, one of the first modern languages to take shape and to be provided with grammatical rules, quickly spread throughout the American continent, where it has remained indelible in almost all of the Central and South American countries. Currently, it is one of the most-spoken languages in the world, with almost 500 million speakers. At present, two other languages originating from Latin are spoken in Spain (the Catalan and the Galician), as well as a Pre-Roman language of unknown origins (the Basque).

Spanish literature has produced geniuses of universal size, whose works have been translated into many languages for several centuries. The most renowned example is Miguel de Cervantes, with his famous work 'Don Quixote', but also authors such as the mystics (Saint) Juan de la Cruz and (Saint) Teresa de Jesús, the bitter and biting Francisco de Quevedo, and the celebrated novelist Benito Pérez Galdós and – more recently – poets such as Antonio Machado, Federico García Lorca, Juan Ramón Jiménez and Vicente Alexandre stand out, the last two having been awarded the Nobel prize.

But it has probably been the painting genre that has expressed the best of Spanish temperament. So it is worth mentioning that, among the classics, painters such as Velázquez and Goya, many of whose paintings, together with those of El Greco, Zurbarán and Murillo, can be admired in the Prado Museum (Madrid), one of the main art galleries in the world. Among the modern painters, Picasso, Dalí and Miró are noteworthy, and more recently Tàpies, Barceló or López must be mentioned. Along with them, it is necessary adding some well-known sculptors like Chillida or Oteiza.

In the architectural and monumental field, Spain enjoys the results of being a multicultural nation with remote historical roots. Signs of Christian art can be found not only in some of its cathedrals (Santiago de Compostela, León, Burgos and Toledo) but also are reflected in many small churches and in some medieval monasteries. There are also beautiful examples of Muslim architecture, such as the palace-fortress of La Alhambra (Granada) and the mosque at Córdoba. There are even valuable remains from the Roman age, as the famous aqueduct at Segovia and the theatre at Mérida. Among the most famous Spanish contemporary architects one must count Moneo (Pritzker Award) and Saénz de Oiza.

However, in the field of music, Spain lacks a rich tradition. In the period of the greatest national splendour (sixteenth century), there were a few celebrated masters, namely, Morales, Guerrero and Victoria. Later, the main Spanish contributions have been in the sphere of popular music, which has played an important role in inspiring many composers, both nationally and internationally. In fact, the 'flamenco' (especially 'cante jondo') is one of the most significant signs of Spanish culture throughout the entire world. In the period between the nineteenth and the twentieth centuries, a musical renaissance involving composers such as Albeniz, Granados and Falla took place, as did the development of its own musical genre, half opera, operetta and theatre, known as 'zarzuela'. Barbieri, Bretón, Chapí and Chueca are some of the most famous creators of zarzuelas.

15. Spain is a country of deep religious tradition, defendant at specific times in its history of a fundamentalist Roman Catholicism. As a result, Spain has for centuries received a mark of religious intolerance but maybe not totally justified. However, it cannot be denied that in 1492 the Catholic Monarchs decided to expel from their kingdoms all Jews who did not convert to Catholicism, as well as – in order to monitor the truthfulness of those conversions – to institute the fearful Inquisition ('Tribunal de la Santa Inquisición'), which committed many abuses in the name of the catholic credo purification.

It must also not be forgotten that Spanish theologians and politicians reacted strongly against the process of the Reformation that Martin Luther led in Germany. They were the main instigators of the Council of Trento, which formed the foundation of the so-called Counter-Reformation. In 1609 the Moorish people – that is, the descendants of Muslims who, as with the Jews, had been obliged to a mandatory conversion to Catholicism at the end of the Reconquest – were also expelled from Spain. Nevertheless, many documents of daily life in medieval Spain offer examples of a peaceful cohabitation among Christians, Jews and Muslims. Also, some of the less dark pages concerning Catholicism history have been written by Spaniards. This was shown in the determined defence of the American Indians' human dignity made by (Friar) Bartolomé de las Casas and the basis for the foundation of the Society of Jesus by (Saint) Ignatius Loyola.

16. Spain has not been a nation especially talented for the cultivation of the sciences, at least not in the last two or three centuries, as scientific development requires a basis of a solid political, social and economic stability, which Spain frequently lacked in that period.

Probably its most remarkable scientific breakthroughs happened during the age of Muslim hegemony, when very important physicians and mathematicians (Avicena, Averroes) lived in Spain. Later, only isolated figures, normally related to medical science, can be mentioned, such as Miguel Servet, who formulated the theory of the double circulation of the blood; Santiago Ramón y Cajal, who made important progress in histology; and Severo Ochoa, an outstanding scientist in the research of the neuronal tissues. Several engineers associated with the creation or improvement of specific devices can also be mentioned, for example, the submarine (Isaac Peral); the dirigible (Torres Quevedo); and the autogiro – a precursor of the helicopter (Ricardo de la Cierva).

17. The Spanish character is finely expressed through popular cultural exhibitions that embrace poetry, music, cuisine, dance, games and festivities. Bullfighting stands out among the festivities and is so linked to the Spanish cultural history that it is frequently called the 'national festivity'. The spectacle is based on a face-to-face fight with a bull, the bullfighter having a piece of red cloth to avoid the bull's charges. The bull is repeatedly harmed during the show to weaken the power of its charges. In the end, the bullfighter must kill the bull, which for years has caused this spectacle to be especially criticized by animal protection lobbies that have demanded that it be prohibited. In July 2010, the Parliament of Catalonia banned bullfighting in Catalonia.

Bullfights appear in almost every popular festival, celebrated at least once a year in Spanish towns, both large and smaller ones, for the commemoration of their respective patrons (i.e., Saint Isidro in Madrid). As a result, the bullring is one of the typical buildings that can be seen in the majority of the Spanish cities. Apart from bullfighting, other famous popular and well-visited festivals in Spain are 'Sanfermines' in Pamplona, 'Fallas' in Valencia and the processions of the Holy Week in Sevilla.

18. Currently, Spain is completely immersed in the European cultural sphere and takes part in the most avant-garde tendencies in the fields of painting, architecture, music, cinema and fashion. There is, as occurs in many other countries, a strong influence of cultural expressions originating in the US, especially those connected with cinema and television, although the Spanish public, given its idiomatic identity, is also very open to cultural products from Central and South America, especially those related to literature and cinema. In the field of cinema, Spain, since the 1980s, has flourished with several stars working in Hollywood studios and some directors, such as P. Almodóvar, being awarded an Oscar for the best non-English language film (*All About My Mother*, 1999) and another one for the best original screenplay (*Talk to Her*, 2002).

In Spain, a mixed TV system is maintained. Besides public-owned channels, there are privately owned ones, although the total number of TV channels that broadcast within the national territory with national coverage and relevant audience is under ten. Both radio and press have a strong tradition in Spain and currently continue to be very powerful tools for constructing public opinion. However, TV is the mass medium with a larger comparative audience (89% of the total population) than radio (55%) and daily press (40%).

The three national newspapers that receive the majority of sales are *El País* (the most influential newspaper published in Spanish and one of the best valued internationally), *ABC* and *El Mundo*. Some sports newspapers also have a large copy edition. The press is available online via Internet, a system of access to information used more and more by the Spaniards: 68% of Spanish households have Internet access, compared to 76% of the EU average, and 67% have broadband access compared to 72% of the European average (Eurostat, 2012).

In the field of sports, football plays the role of 'national sport' in Spain, not only because it is played a great deal by amateurs but also because professional football is massively supported. In fact, some of the most internationally prestigious football clubs (Real Madrid, Barcelona FC) are Spanish, and Spain was the winner of the football world championship 2010. Athletics is another rising sport, particularly events such as the marathon and the 1,500 m flat race. Obviously its rise is being related to the surge to Spanish sport achieved as a result of the 1992 Olympic Games being held in Barcelona. Other sports often played in Spain, and in which Spanish sportsmen and sportswomen frequently excel, are tennis, sailing, golf, water polo and cycling. This last one even has an annual inescapable appointment in Spain, because one of the three unique three-week cycling competitions (the 'Vuelta') is run here.

§3. Political System

19. Spain is currently a kingdom, articulated according to the form of state known as 'parliamentary monarchy'. The King of Spain since 1975, when General Franco's regime concluded, is Juan Carlos I of Bourbon. The role that the king plays is Head of State, with mainly symbolic functions. Spain has a political Constitution, enacted in 1978. It embodies the classical principle of separation of powers, as well as respect for a series of civil rights and freedoms. It is an advanced Constitution, with a clear concern for guaranteeing several principles related to the 'Welfare State'. It also incorporates the essential principle of non-discrimination with respect to sex, race, religion, ideology or any other personal condition.

The legislative power is assigned to a parliament ('Cortes'), divided into two Houses ('Congreso' and 'Senado'), whose main function is the preparation and enactment of the laws as well as, once a year, the approval of the State General Budget. The executive power is carried out by the Government, which consists of the Premier and a varying number of ministers. Among its functions must be mentioned those of submitting bills for Cortes' approval and laying down regulations (i.e., rules developing laws). Taking into account the fact that Spain is a monarchy, there is not a system for the presidential election of the Prime Minister, but he/she is indirectly elected by the Cortes. The public Administration, which is linked to and conducted by the Government, enjoys a huge staff and powerful economic means. Following the French model, the Spanish public Administration has significant functions and prerogatives.

In Spain, the judicial power is in the hands of professional judges who take up their posts after passing an unbiased selection test. The judicial organization is still relatively complex in spite of the recent efforts developed in order to achieve greater simplification. The judicial structuring is based on a division of issues according to four jurisdictional fields (civil, criminal, administrative and labour issues). As a rule, there is the possibility of making an appeal against the sentence pronounced by any judge. In some cases, depending on the issue and the amount of the litigation, there is subsequently the possibility of making a high court appeal. The court that hears it, that is to say, the highest court in the Spanish judicial structure, is called the Supreme Court ('Tribunal Supremo' (TS)). For defined criminal trials only, the intervention of a jury is foreseen in Spain.

The monitoring of laws in accordance with constitutional provisions, as well as the function of correcting possible infringements of civil rights, is entrusted to a specialized entity, called Constitutional Court ('Tribunal Constitucional' (TC)). Therefore, in Spain a system of 'judicial review' is not applied, but rather a concentrated system of constitutional justice, similar to those in Germany and Italy.

20. From a territorial point of view, Spain is organized in a way very similar to that of a Federal State, with a state (or 'federal') power and several territorial entities endowed with political autonomy. These entities are called Autonomous Communities ('Comunidades Autónomas') (CC AA). Some of them (Navarre, Catalonia, Valencia and Balearic Islands) coincide with regions that in the past enjoyed independence as kingdoms separated from Castile, the central and largest region in Spain, the kingdom that historically polarized around itself the national unity since the conquest of America in 1492. The episode of the Succession War (*see supra* paragraph 12) fed the nationalism feeling in some regions such as Catalonia, Aragon, Valencia and Balearic Islands, while other subsequent events caused a similar effect in areas such as the Basque Country and Navarre. The nationalism feeling, and even the desire of independency observable in some Spanish regions, was completely neutralized during General Franco's dictatorial regime, which was obviously established on deeply centralist foundations. With the arrival of the new regime of political freedoms, it is not unusual that, since 1975, the topic of nationalism is at the forefront of the public debate.

The CC AA model, inserted into the Constitution of 1978 was intended as a compromise solution that, without sacrificing the national territorial unity, permitted satisfaction to the political autonomy requested by certain regions. The model is based on an open system of distribution of competences. Except for a certain catalogue of issues that are exclusively assigned to the ('federal') State, the rest may be assumed by the CC AA. Even within the catalogue of state-exclusive competences, some of them may be conveyed to the CC AA, which has frequently occurred in the last few years. In the field of Civil Law, the exclusive legislative competence belongs to the State, without prejudice to the preservation, modification and development by the CC AA of their statutory provisions, where they exist. In any case, the legislative power of this closed catalogue of matters, belongs exclusively to the State: rules concerning the implementation and effectiveness of legal norms, civil legal relations concerning the forms of marriage, keeping of records and public instruments, bases of contractual obligations, rules for resolving conflicts of laws and determination of the sources of law, with respect, in the latter case, to the special provisions of the CC AA (Article 149.1.8 of CE).

Generally speaking, the model has worked well and has granted the CC AA a degree of autonomy even higher than that enjoyed by similar territorial entities in other countries (*länder* in Germany or cantons in Switzerland). However, in some CC AA, violent groups continued to brandish the flag of independency as a fallacious alibi to justify their purely terrorist activities. Such has been the case of the Basque Country and the terrorist group ETA, responsible for killing more than 800 people for four decades of activity, until the 20 October 2011, on which ETA announced a definitive cessation of its armed activity. The effective dissolution of all ETA's structures has been confirmed on 3 May 2018.

Since 2012 it has gained momentum in Catalonia a strong independence movement previously unknown, driven by regional parties of varied ideological orientations. After a mock referendum conducted in November 2014, which was declared invalid by the TC, in the regional elections of September 2015 supporters of independence or of a referendum about this possibility won most seats in the regional chamber, but not most votes at the polls. Nevertheless, the regional president felt committed to going ahead with the sovereignty process. After two years of growing tension and lack of dialogue with the central government, former regional president, Carles Puigdemont, supported by the majority of the regional parliamentary chamber, decided to call a referendum, declared illegal and suspended by the TC. Nevertheless, the referendum took place de facto on 1 October 2017, although the police forces dismantled many polling stations by court order. Neither international observers or political organizations nor other countries considered that the referendum had met international standards. According to the final results (announced by the Catalan government itself), with a participation of 43.03%, there were 2.020.144 affirmative votes against 176.565 negative votes (to the question 'Do you want Catalonia to be an independent state in the form of a republic?'). However, these results were not ratified by any neutral body and widely questioned both for the irregularities during the day of the vote and for the lack of coherence with the previous provisional results.

On 27 October 2017, following the results of the referendum, the Parliament of Catalonia approved a declaration of Catalonia as an independent Republic, by secret ballot and with the absence of all opposition deputies. The declaration of independence was suspended four days later by the TC. On the same day, October 27, at the request of the Government, the Senate approved the dismissal of the Catalan government and announced anticipated regional elections. The attorney general requested the arrest and prosecution of former President Puigdemont and other former members of the Catalan government for sedition, rebellion and embezzlement of public funds. Several of them were put in provisional prison awaiting trial and others fled from Spanish justice in several European countries. The process continues before the TS (the trial was opened on 12 February 2019). After the regional elections of December 2017 the most-voted party was the most anti-independence one, but the sum of deputies of the pro-independence parties allowed again the appointment of a regional president of pro-independence trend. Although the new regional government seems less inclined to commit transgressions of the constitutional order, the lack of understanding with the central government continues and the social confrontation is increasing.

21. Traditionally, in Spain only two large national political parties so far had had a real possibility of governing, should an electoral process took place: the Conservative party ('Partido Popular'), and the social-democratic one ('Partido Socialista Obrero Español'). Additional parties included a left wing party with scarce representation (less than 10%) and a few parties of nationalist tendency that obtain representation only in electoral districts corresponding to the territories of their respective CC AA. This relatively simple scene contrasted with the huge quantity and variety of political parties that concurred with the first free elections held in Spain after General Franco's regime (1977).

However, since mid-2011 a significant citizen movement emerged (referred to as 15-M Movement, or 'Indignados' Movement), highly critical of the traditional political parties, calling for a democratic regeneration. The outcome of the General Elections of 20 December 2015 inaugurated a new historical era in Spanish politics, characterized by the end of the traditional two-parties system and the emergence of at least two new parties: one on the far left ('Podemos') and another one on the soft right ('Ciudadanos'). Both of them have obtained a remarkable representation in the Spanish Parliament due to the votes from people disappointed with the classic parties. Any future government to be formed will probably be the fruit of an agreement between two or more parties, given the difficulty that an isolated party obtains enough majority of the Congress.

In the period between 1977 and 2015, three political parties have governed the nation: a centrist political party, which has already disappeared, led by Adolfo Suárez and Leopoldo Calvo-Sotelo (1977–1982); the Conservative party, first under the leadership of José María Aznar (1996–2004), and then under the leadership of Mariano Rajoy (2011–2018); and the Social-Democratic party, led in a first stage by Felipe González (1982–1996), in a second stage by José Luis Rodríguez Zapatero (2004–2011) and ultimately by Pedro Sánchez (2018), current Premier of the Spanish Government after a vote for non-confidence against former Premier Mariano Rajoy on 1 June 2018. General elections were called for on 28 April 2019.

Chapter 2. Legal Background of the Country

§1. Legal Family or Tradition

22. Spain, in view of its geographical location and its cultural and political tradition, is undoubtedly included among the so-called Western Law countries, namely, the European ones (maybe not with complete clearness in the case of Russia and other Eastern Europe countries); the whole of America (except Cuba); Australia; New Zealand; and South Africa. The Western Law is also significantly present in Japan, the Asiatic Southeast, several African countries, Israel and some other Middle East countries.

Western Law, as opposed to Islamic Law, African Consuetudinary Law, Far East Law (China, India) and 'Sovietic inspiration' Law (Cuba, North Korea), is characterized by an individualistic conception of the social order, based on the idea that every individual has an inherent ability to hold rights. This individualism implies a deep liberalism that leads to the organization of a strong judicial protection for civil rights against the action of public powers. Western Law is also characterized by a secular approach to the State.

In Western Law countries, Law and not religion (or any other 'system of rules') is the most important method of social control as well as the most powerful way toward social progress. Above all, Western Law countries constitute States being subject to Law and are based on the separation of powers. Moreover, in the Western Law countries, the law,[2] on the understanding that it is the purest expression of people's sovereignty expressed by means of a parliament, is the centrepiece of what the Law system is all about.

23. There are two juridical families, or traditions, known predominately within Western Law: Roman Law – also called Civil Law or Continental Law – and Common Law (or Anglo-Saxon Law). While the former is deeply influenced by the medieval revival of the Roman Law (i.e., particularly, Emperor Justinian's *Corpus Juris Civilis*), the doctrines of the rationalist school of Natural Law and the codification, those influences have been much weaker in the latter, its main mark of identity being the value of the body of law built by the courts throughout the ages, case after case.

As opposed to Civil Law lawyers, who show a strong tendency to formulate abstract principles and to worry seriously about scientific system building, Common Law lawyers have a casuistic rather than a dogmatic point of view and concern themselves with solving problems effectively. Finally, in a Civil Law system, there is a clearer separation between substantive and procedural laws.

Despite everything, the two Western Law families tend to converge, and the differences between them have been greatly reduced in the late decades. This phenomenon is due first to the approval of many international conventions and uniform laws on specific issues (patents, copyright, and international sale of goods, international

2. That is to say, the 'written law' or the 'statute'.

transport of passengers/goods), which has caused an unavoidable rapprochement between the systems of the countries involved.

Second, it must be mentioned that a deep legislative harmonization has been taking place between the UK and the rest of State Members of the EU. Third, many typical institutions from one of the Western Law traditions have been adopted by the other. Thus, not only the increasing role of the precedent system in Civil Law countries and the adoption of traditional institutions from the English Law such as trust can be observed, but also, and by contrast, the daily growth of Statute Law is noticeable in Common Law countries.

24. Spanish Law – as does of the French, the Germans and the Italians – belongs to the Civil Law tradition. Spain, whose territory had been part of the legendary Roman Empire, quickly supported the work of studying and interpreting the classical and post-classical Roman jurisconsults' texts, particularly Emperor Justinian's *Corpus Juris Civilis*.[3]

Besides the Roman Law revival, a new Law appeared in Spain, first with a local character and later, starting with the birth of the modern State (sixteenth century), with a national character. From the end of the fifteenth century until the mid-eighteenth century, coinciding with the greatest splendour of the absolute monarchy, so many rules were produced that large legal compilations needed to be elaborated.[4]

At the end of the eighteenth century, Europe witnessed the downfall of the *Ancien Régime*, as well as the birth of new forms of political and legal organizations based on the ideology of the Enlightenment and the rationalist school of Natural Law. By breaking up its old moulds, the Continental Law started to be thoroughly codified. The codification tried to solve exhaustively all the hypothetical conflicts relating to a defined matter by means of *ratione materiae* homogeneous laws based on a systematic and structured method, as well as being expressed in simple terms.

The first codes made in accordance with these parameters saw the light of day in France, but one did not have to be kept waiting too long in Spain. First of all, the Criminal Code (1822) and the Commercial Code (Ccom) (1829) were enacted, although both have since been replaced. However, the Civil Code (CC) was not passed until 1889, mainly because of the multiplicity of civil legal provisions peculiar to various Spanish regions (Catalonia, Navarre, Aragon, Basque Country, Galicia and Balearic Islands). This CC, with many subsequent reforms, is still in force.

25. During the twentieth century, the Civil Law-tradition countries moved away from the codification model. It is often said that one lives in the age of the 'decodification' or 'post-codification'. Codes have proved to be an inadequate instrument for regulating the complex and variable reality of modern society. Therefore special

3. This work had begun in the twelfth century at the universities of North Italy.
4. In Spain, the most celebrated of these compilations during the reign of Felipe II was the so-called New Compilation, dated 1567.

laws meant to cover every different field (consumers' protection, insurance contracts, human-assisted reproduction, and joint ownership of blocks of flats), are being passed in an ever-increasing proportion.

The twentieth century has also been the century of the birth of new branches of the Law, such as the Labour Law, currently totally endowed with undoubted autonomy in countries belonging to the Continental Law tradition. In Spain, the principal issues related to the rights of workers and to the work contract are ruled in a special law named 'Statute of Workers'. Moreover, in the Civil Law-family countries, there has been an increased development in administrative laws (laws on education; public health; exploitation of roads, harbours, and coasts; exploitation of forestry, mining, and hydric resources; and environment protection), a phenomenon connected with the coming of the Welfare State.

26. In the sphere of Constitutional Law, countries belonging to the Civil Law tradition – and Spain is not the exception – are characterized by being endowed with a written Constitution wherein the acknowledgement of a series of individual rights and freedoms is solemnly declared. Also the constitution describes the composition, powers, and basic functions of each and every State entity. In countries such as Spain, which has a complex territorial structure – that is to say, with regional entities endowed with political autonomy – the Constitution also deals with the distribution of competences among the (federal) State and the autonomous territorial entities.[5]

The history of constitutions is relatively recent, beginning with the French and American Revolutions at the end of the eighteenth century. In Spain, the first Constitution was passed in 1812, during the Independence War against the Napoleonic troops. Subsequently, five other constitutions have been passed (1837, 1845, 1869, 1876, and 1931), until arriving at the present one, dating from 1978.

As indicated above, and as is typical in Civil Law countries, Spain does not follow a system of 'judicial review' but a concentrated system of constitutional justice, which means that the function of checking the constitutionality of the ordinary laws is assigned to the TC a specialized organ named 'TC' (Articles 159–165 CE). Nevertheless, the control of the constitutionality of governmental regulations may be carried out by ordinary judges and tribunals, without the need for introducing a question (of constitutionality) before the TC. The same occurs with the laws that came into force prior to the Constitution (29 December 1978). The TC is, however, the highest guardian of respect by the public authorities for individual rights and freedoms. To that end, every time a citizen feels that some public authority has encroached upon one of his/her fundamental rights,[6] he/she may give notice of a special appeal before the TC,[7] provided that he/she has previously asked for protection before the ordinary judges and tribunals and that all the ordinary ways of appeal or high court appeal have been exhausted. The TC is also in charge of resolving the conflicts concerning competences between the (federal) State and the CC AA.

---

5. In Spain, as said above, these entities are called Autonomous Communities (CC AA).
6. That is to say, one of the rights whose protection is foreseen in Arts 14–30 CE.
7. This appeal is known as 'protection appeal' (in Spanish, *recurso de amparo*).

The CE is a rigid one because a complex procedure of reform has been foreseen, very different from the one for ordinary laws. Actually, the Constitution procedure of reform is two-fold: If the intention is to make a total revision of the Constitution or to modify some of its specially strategic chapters,[8] then the process includes the Cortes' approval by a two-thirds majority, the dissolution of both legislative Houses, the ratifying agreement of each of the newly elected Houses, and the subsequent ratification by means of a referendum. In any other case, the approval of both Houses by a three-fifths majority will be enough.

27. Despite the apparent unity that reigns over the Civil Law-tradition countries, there are remarkable differences among them. It is possible to make a division between German tradition countries (Germany, Austria, and Switzerland) and Latin-tradition countries (France, Italy, and Spain). The differences are noticeable in several aspects related to the patrimonial Private Law,[9] and more specifically to those related to the system of acquisition and publicity of property rights.

For example, in German tradition countries, a system of constitutive registration for the conveyance of immovable property rights is in function. Apart from that, the whole Land Registry organization is designed on the basis of the principle of protection for the appearance created by the Registry. However, in France and Italy, the principle of non-opposability of non-registered property rights prevails. In Spain, as explained below, a mixed system, partly influenced by the German tradition and partly by the Latin one, applies.

Also, in Germany a system of acquisition of property rights based on an abstract conveying agreement is applicable. This kind of agreement is totally disconnected, from a 'causal' point of view, with the juridical act (e.g., contract) by means of which one of the contracting parties conveys to the other the right at issue. Contrary to this, in Latin-tradition countries there is always a causal link between the conveying juridical act (e.g., contract), that generates the obligation to alienate the right in question and the conveyance *stricto sensu* of that right to the extent that, in French and in Italian Law, the alienation takes place automatically by the mere fact of putting the conveying contract into proper form. In Spain, as described below, it is necessary to combine an acquisition title (e.g., a contract of sale),[10] and a conveyance method, that is, the possessory transfer of the goods that are the object of alienation (Article 609 CC),[11] in such a way that any vicissitudes that affect the title can have repercussions on the whole conveyance mechanism.

One more field in which there is a noticeable difference between German and Latin Civil Law countries is the one relating to the marriage economic relations. Although in German Law tradition a system currently prevails in which every spouse is entitled to a deferred sharing in the profits of the other when the marriage

8. Such as the one that defines the monarchic form of the State or the one that contains the acknowledgement of the fundamental civil rights.
9. 'The accepted major classifications of law within the civil law tradition are public law and private law. Within private law there are two main fields: civil law and commercial law.' *See* J.H. Merryman, *The Civil Law Tradition* 68 (Stanford University Press 2d ed. 1985). Within public law are included the constitutional law, the administrative law, and the criminal law (addition ours).
10. Which in Spanish is called *título*.
11. Which in Spanish is called *modo*.

is over, the Latin Law countries' typical system is one of marriage partnership, by virtue of which the spouses are co-owners of everything that they both acquire during the marriage by means of their work (*see* Spain Article 1316 CC).

The way of ruling the ordinary co-ownership is also very different. In the German Law-tradition countries, there is a type of co-ownership without individual detachable and conveyable quotas, whereas in the Latin-tradition countries, the legal model of co-ownership is reminiscent of the Roman Law classical one: detachability of individual abstract quotas and the ability of any co-owner to convey his/her quota in favour of a third party (*see* Spain Article 399 CC).

Finally, an important contrast in the matter of Successory Law should be noted. The strong predominance of the principle of individual testamentary freedom characterizes the Latin Law family, but in the German Law tradition, individuals (normally spouses) are allowed to make joint testaments, or even to reach successory agreements (normally between close relatives). Moreover, contrary to the German system of automatic acquisition of an inheritance, in Latin-tradition countries such as Spain, the acquisition of an inheritance depends on an express juridical act of acceptance by every inheritor (*see* Articles 988 et seq. CC).

§2. Relation and Hierarchy Between the Sources of Law

28. The highest level of rule within the Spanish legal order is the Constitution passed in 1978. In accordance with the predominant tendency within the current constitutional theory, CE has a direct legal efficacy, which means that its articles are compulsory per se, although they have still not been developed by subsequent rules (Article 9.1 CE). Its contents, especially those related to the acknowledgement of a series of individual rights and freedoms (Articles 14 et seq. CE), are therefore the first source of law, and they constitute an obligatory reference to which any remaining rules must be adjusted. If contrary to the Constitutional arrangements, laws and regulations can be ruled unconstitutional and consequently invalid.

29. Under the Constitution, the main source of Law in Spain is the legislative law (statutes enacted by legislature). This is, however, a complex category, within which several types may be differentiated. The law *par excellence* is the one passed by parliament.[12] The CE relates in specific detail the procedure of preparation of a statute (Articles 81–92 CE). The most significant matters (e.g., the development of individual rights and freedoms, the electoral rules, the procedure for calling a referendum, and the organization of the TC) must be regulated by means of special laws, named 'organic laws', which are characterized thus because the passing of them requires the affirmative vote of the absolute majority among the members of the Congress. The rest of the laws, whose passing does not require this special majority, are named 'ordinary laws'.

Sometimes, the Government may enact rules endowed with the same force as parliamentary statutes. These rules, which are not allowed to deal with specific matters

12. In Spain, as said above, the parliament – called the Cortes – consists of two Houses: Congress and Senate.

and have to be justified by the state of urgency, are called decree-laws, and they must be ratified by the Congress within a term of thirty days following their approval. It can also be seen that the Government promulgates other kinds of rules endowed with the force of law, namely acting by virtue of the Cortes' delegation. For this, two modalities are used.

First, it is possible that the Cortes enact a 'law of bases' and afterwards delegate the Government to develop those bases through a so-called articled text. Second, the Cortes have the option to authorize the Government to reduce to a sole corpus (named 'recast text') several laws existing upon a specific matter. In both cases, when the Government acts by virtue of the Cortes' authorization, the resulting statute is officially named 'legislative decree'.

However, it must not be forgotten that in Spain the CC AA are also competent to enact their own laws. With this aim in mind, all of them have a 'legislative assembly' made of members elected in exactly the same manner as the members of the state Congress and Senate. The laws enacted by the CC AA, which are known as 'autonomic laws', must deal with matters within the scope of their respective competences in accordance with what the Constitution foresees in this respect (Articles 148–149 CE). Between autonomic laws and state laws, a hierarchical relationship is not to be found, but a scope one. Therefore, both kinds of laws have the same force, and any eventual conflict between them must be solved by the TC on the basis of deciding to which entity the competence belongs. It must be noted that six CC AA retain some degree of legislative competence in the field of Civil Law, in view of their historical provisions in this field. The CE respects their power to legislate provided that it is exercised within the scope defined by Article 149.1.8 CE, which gives the State the exclusive legislative power on a closed catalogue of matters (*see supra* paragraph 20). All of those six CC AA have enacted laws on civil matters (normally provisions on inheritance relations and economic relations between spouses). In the case of Catalonia, several parts of a complete CC have been enacted between 2002 and 2010. The fifth part is devoted to the regulation of property and other real rights.

Nevertheless, there is a hierarchical relationship between the laws (either state or autonomic ones) and the governmental regulations (either given by the national Government or given by one of the autonomic governments). All the regulations must abide by the laws, of which they merely constitute a development. In Spain, every regulation approved by the state (or federal) Government is named 'royal decree'.

Rules endowed with the force of law must include the sentences of the TC that declare unconstitutional, totally or partly, a law. They have, although in an inverted sense, the same kind of efficacy as the law whose unconstitutionality they declare.

All the rules having the force of law, in view of their general efficacy, are the subject of publication in the State Official Gazette, which includes the sentences of the TC. Unless they foresee something else, their coming into force takes place twenty days after the final publication in the State Official Gazette (Article 2.1 CC).

30. In addition to the law *lato sensu*,[13] there are two other sources of Law in Spain: custom and the so-called general principles of Law. With regard to custom, custom is admitted only as a suppletory source, for lack of law[14] or when the law itself refers expressly to a custom. A custom, if alleged during a process, must be proved as a matter of fact, which means that the maxim *iura novit curia* is not applicable to custom, unlike statutes or regulations. The custom has its main, but small, scope in some fields within the Civil and the Commercial Law, especially in relation to certain contracts.

As regards the general principles of Law, they function at the same time as a suppletory source of Law, for lack of both law and custom, and as instruments for the interpretation of the provisions of the other sources of Law, in order to make the judicial application of the statutory – and, on a smaller scale, customary – rules easier. The main difficulty in relation to them is fixing their definite content because they are not always expressly articled in a legal corpus, and when they are, their profiles are often not well defined. Therefore, the scope of the general principles of Law is slowly being specified by the jurisprudence,[15] which implies a significant amount of legal uncertainty.

Some of the general principles of Law are expressly articled, even in the CE, for example, the principle of non-discrimination or equality before the Law (Article 14 CE) and the principles of legality, hierarchy among legal rules, publicity of the Law, and non-arbitrariness of public powers (Article 9.3 CE). Others are stated in the CC, that is, the principle of exercising rights according to the parameters of good faith (Article 7.1 CC); the principle that forbids the misuse of subjective rights (Article 7.2 CC); the principle that recognizes the power of individuals to regulate their own interests in the field of private law; and specifically in the field of contracts, best known as 'principle of autonomy of the will' (Article 1255 CC); the principle *pacta sunt servanda* (Articles 1091 and 1258 CC)[16] and the principle *alterum non laedere* (Articles 1902 et seq. CC).[17] Judges and tribunals often apply these principles and sometimes a few others not necessarily connected with determined legal provisions, that is, the principle *nemo plus iura transferre potest quam ipse habet* or the principle that forbids *contra factum proprium venire.*[18]

31. The term *jurisprudence* is used in Spanish to mean the whole of the sentences pronounced by judges and tribunals and, more specifically, the whole of the sentences pronounced by the TS. In the Spanish system, jurisprudence is not a source of Law. According to Article 1.6 CC, the function of jurisprudence is to be a complement to the legal order. Thus, the sentences of the TS do not result from an

13. That is to say, the parliamentary statutes, the legislation having the force of law promulgated by the executive order under delegated powers, and even the governmental regulations.
14. Therefore, provided that 'there is no applicable statute or regulation to the contrary'. *See* J.H. Merryman, *The Civil Law Tradition* 23 (Stanford University Press 2d ed. 1985).
15. For the exact meaning of the term *jurisprudence* in Spain and, in general, in the Civil Law tradition countries, *see infra* immediately.
16. In other words: 'the agreements must be kept'.
17. In other words: 'every damage caused to another person must be indemnified'.
18. That is to say, respectively, 'nobody may convey a right that he/she does not hold', and 'nobody may lawfully act against his/her own previous actions'.

activity of creating new rules but from interpreting and applying the existing ones. The TS, contrary to what happens in other countries in which the rule of stare decisis prevails, is not compelled by its own prior decisions in such a way that, although there is a precedent, it may dissociate from it. Likewise, lower judges and tribunals are not compelled by their own prior decisions nor by the jurisprudence of the TS, although they are obviously influenced by the last one. Certainly, if a judge dissociates from the jurisprudence of the TS, it is possible to file a high court appeal based on this fact, but the judge cannot be prosecuted because of infringing the Law, as could be the case if he/she had dissociated him/herself from statutory provisions.

32. In order to complete the catalogue of sources of Law, it is necessary to refer to, on the one hand, international treaties and, on the other hand, 'derivative' legislation made in the bosom of the EU, to which Spain, since 1986, belongs. As regards international treaties, after they have been agreed to in the proper form and officially publicized in Spain, they are endowed with a force higher than the law, thus their provisions cannot be modified nor derogated unless in accordance with the treaties themselves and with the general rules of International Law (Article 96.1 CE). For the approval of some kinds of treaties (i.e., military ones or ones that affect the territorial integrity of Spain), the Government must previously obtain the permission of the Cortes.

With regard to the European Law, insofar as the Member States of the EU have made a conveyance of sovereignty in favour of the European institutions, the results of the legislative activity of these do not have a conditional validity, but a definitive one. An internal act of official publication in every Member State is not necessary. The European 'laws' are the object of publication in the EU Official Gazette. After they have been publicized, they come into force, every one of them in accordance with the degree of efficacy described in the constituent treaties. From a hierarchical point of view, the European TS of Justice has repeatedly established the principle of primacy of the European Law over the internal Law of every Member State.

Chapter 3. Introduction to the Law of Property and Trust

33. Some preliminary comments are necessary before making a study of the contents of this chapter. Although the original title suggested for this section in the General Outlines of the *International Encyclopaedia of Laws* has been maintained, it is not usual to talk about 'property and trust' in Spanish Law but about 'property and other real rights'. In Spain, as occurs in the rest of the Civil Law-tradition countries, the trust, as will be seen in detail below, is not an institution that is actually the object of legal treatment.

34. The expression 'real rights' (from the Latin *res-rei* = thing) must be simply understood as 'rights in things'.[19] Among them, property is undoubtedly the clearest example. In Spanish Law, the matter relative to real rights constitutes a part of the Civil Law, more specifically a part of the 'patrimonial Civil Law'.

The other major section within the patrimonial Civil Law is the Law on contracts and obligations. Nevertheless, in Spanish Law it is possible to find not only real rights but also rights of credit either in movable or in immovable goods. In other words, the goods, to whichever class they belong, can be the object of both 'real' legal relations and 'obligatory' legal relations.

35. In the same way that the real rights are absolute rights, the rights of credit are relative ones. Although absolute rights such as real rights do, give the owner a power that he/she can exercise against all others (*erga omnes* efficacy), relative rights, such as the rights of credit do, guarantee the owner a power that he/she can use only against one or more determined persons (*inter partes* efficacy). Moreover, the owner of a property right or any other right in a thing,[20] unlike the holder of a right of credit, can directly obtain the benefits that the thing at issue is able to produce, without need for a determined person (i.e., a debtor or obligor) to render any performance in his/her favour.[21]

§1. Historical Origins and Evolution

36. Property and other real rights have the same origin and evolution in Spain as in other Civil Law countries. If one looks to the past, everything seems to indicate that in the Antiquity, there was no concept of private property as is currently known. All goods belonged to the community. In Rome, as later among Germanic peoples,

19. 'Things' is the literal translation. In the text we will refer mostly to 'goods' or 'object', however.
20. Although property attributes full sovereignty over the thing that constitutes its object, the other real rights give only a limited sovereignty. Because of that, the real rights other than property are known as 'limited real rights', or 'real rights in another person's goods' (*iura in re aliena*).
21. According to Merryman, in the field of real rights, 'the immediate relation between the man and the thing stands out clearly, and is effective without need for cooperation of others. Other subjects must merely abstain from interfering in the peaceful exercise of this sovereignty. In an obligatory relation, however (where only relative rights are involved), the conduct of another subject who is held to a determined conduct is of primary importance.' *See* J.H. Merryman, *The Civil Law Tradition* 74 (Stanford University Press 2d ed. 1985).

the concept of private property developed initially with regard to the movables of quotidian use (foods, clothes, arms, tools). Only with the appearance of the big rural municipal areas in Rome, during the decadence of the Roman Empire, arose a concept of immovable private property, to a certain extent similar to the one that would be known in the Modern Age, although with some connotations of political sovereignty (*dominium quiritarium*). In provinces such as Hispania, property in land belonged to the *princeps* or to the *populus*, but in both cases, it was liable to conveyance in favour of individuals in exchange for a levy.

Gradually, the various kinds of property were brought closer together, until all of them were joined in a sole concept within Emperor Justinian's *Corpus Juris Civilis* (sixth century). According to that concept, property consists of an absolute and exclusive right that embraces, in an abstract sense, every possible action of its owner. This exercise of abstraction did not occur in the Germanic area, where every use that the goods, specifically the immovable ones, were able to have continued to be contemplated separately.

37. During the Middle Ages, property in land, undoubtedly endowed with the greatest economic significance, was subjected to various kinds of entailment that interfered with its free sale or its use as a guarantee. In this way, the currency of wealth was seriously blocked, insofar as there was almost no land for sale, and there was no possibility of securing a debt by means of a mortgage.

The first kind of entailment of land took place in the field of family and was known as 'entailed estate'. The assets that composed an entailed estate, therefore belonging at all times to the first-born son in the family, could not be freely sold outside the family circle. These assets had to be preserved forever in the bosom of the family.

Second, there was the entailment that concerned the estates of ecclesiastical corporations. The Canon Law forbade that the estates acquired by the Church (normally by means of parishioners' legacies and donations) or by any of its members were alienated or encumbered. Because of this, those estates were said to be mortmain, that is to say, in unserviceable hands.

The third kind of entailment concerned the communal character of many estates, whose exploitation was necessarily collective, which therefore impeded their appropriation individually and consequently either their alienation or their encumbrance. Such was the case with meadows, woods, mountains, roads, rivers, channels, bridges, markets and fountains. The process of reconquest and subsequent repopulation of many areas during the Middle Ages gave rise to a great number of this kind of communal estates in Spain because of the understandable need for granting a minimum of welfare to the inhabitants in the new settlements.

38. Against all those kinds of entailments, including the privileges and personal subjections linked to property in land (feudalism), a movement called the bourgeois revolutionary movement took place in several European countries (France, Spain, Belgium, and Italy) from the end of the eighteenth century until the mid-nineteenth century. The newly emerging social class (the bourgeoisie) needed to obtain the means of production, starting with real estate, and to have available solid-enough guarantees to support its members' large amounts of debts, as well.

The new bourgeois model of property was based on the rationalistic ideology upheld by encyclopaedists and partisans of the Enlightenment. The culture medium of that ideology, which was located in France, started in 1789 and involved a series of social and political upheavals, which became known as the 'French Revolution'. However, after an initial period of violence and radical measures, a point of balance was reached between the defenders of the status quo and the promoters of the change. That point of balance was to be seen even in France, where, first, Napoleon's ascent to power and, second, the restoration of the monarchy meant a clear impasse for the revolutionary process. In the beginning, therefore, the complete abolishment of the *Ancien Régime* was rather formal than actual. Nevertheless, during the nineteenth century, enough privileges were abolished and enough estates disentailed to permit the economic and political expansion of the bourgeoisie. Proof of this expansion is, in Spain, the laws on disentailment that foresaw the elimination of the entailed estates in the bosom of the families as well as the compulsory sale of the ecclesiastical estates, which caused serious disputes between the Catholic Church and the governing class. Among those laws, the two most significant are known by the surname of the ministers who proposed them: Mendizábal (19 February 1836) and Madoz (1 May 1855).

39. Contrary to the *Ancien Régime* model of property, the bourgeois model of property is an individual and free one – 'individual' because the things may belong to individuals and not necessarily to the community, the family, the ecclesiastical order, or the guild – and 'free' not only because the property is already not subject to limits that interfere with its conveyance or encumbrance but also because it belongs to free individuals, competent to have the use of their respective goods without obstructions.

This bourgeois and liberal model of property materialized for the first time in the French CC (also known as 'Napoleon Code'), enacted in 1804. Its Article 544 of the French CC defined 'ownership' as the right to use and enjoy a thing in the most absolute way, provided that the owner does not use it in a way forbidden by laws or regulations.

Almost a century later, Article 348 of the Spanish CC contained a very similar definition: 'Property is the right to enjoy and dispose of a thing, within the limits established by law.' Besides this provision, the Spanish CC shows a clear tendency to a model of property as free and disentailed as possible. As a result, the right of usufruct is shaped as a non-perpetual one (Articles 513, 515, and 640 CC), the number of successory substitutions is limited (Article 781 CC), the scope of the conveyance prohibitions is restricted (Article 785.2 CC), and the partition of a thing held in indivision is favoured (Article 400 CC).

40. Gradually, the bourgeois-liberal model of property evolved during the nineteenth and twentieth centuries. Contrary to its initial absolute and unlimited character, the idea stating that property must not only be useful to the owner, but it must also serve to a lesser or a greater extent to the public interest won force. In fact, the right of property has evolved into a kind of right that is deeply controlled and interfered with by the action of the public powers. Nevertheless, unlike the limitations on property that existed in the *Ancien Régime*, the modern limitations are foreseen by the law, which derives from the democratic expression of the people, and are not the result of an act imposed by the privileged class in order to preserve the status quo.

41. The modern concept of property has been clearly reflected in the CE enacted in 1978. On the one hand, Article 33 CE declares the right of private property and of inheritance but subsequently states that this right will be limited by the laws in accordance with its 'social function'. Stating that property must fulfil a social function means that it is not a right exclusively conceived for the owner's benefit but rather that it has a complex status in which general interests are counted in such a way that besides the traditional *ius utendi*, *ius fruendi*, and *ius disponendi*, the owner must carry out a series of duties that is linked to his/her status as owner and must guarantee that his/her exploitation of the thing that is the object of ownership will also be advantageous to the community.[22]

The old paradigm of ownership, shaped under the presumption that it is free as a rule, the limitations being contemplated as the exception, opened the way to a new paradigm according to which the limits to the owner's right are not contingent anymore but have structural limits. As a last resort, the property may be subject to expropriation, which constitutes the clearest example of limitation. Article 33 CE states that 'nobody can be deprived of his/her goods unless a justified cause exists of public utility or social interest, in accordance with the legal provisions and by means of the corresponding compensation'. Nevertheless, the expropriation as a limit to the right of property was already foreseen in Article 349 CC because the Spanish CC is an overdue one. In fact, the matter relative to expropriation has been the subject of a special law ('Law on Compulsory Expropriation') that, although passed much before the Constitution (16 December 1954), is still in force.[23]

42. A significant parameter concerning the sizing up of the scope of the right of property lies in the nature of the object to which it refers. Actually, there is a clear relationship between this parameter and the social function of property because if what is wanted is assuring the collective usefulness of goods, it is obvious that the usefulness of all kinds of goods depends on their respective nature. Consequently, instead of a unitary concept of property, it is more appropriate to speak of several, every one of them endowed with a different type of social function.

This point of view has been confirmed by Sentence of the Constitutional Court (STC) 37/1987 (26 March 1987), which decided an appeal on constitutionality relative to an autonomic law on agrarian reform. It stated that:

> private property (…), has suffered in our century a deep transformation that impedes continuing to think of it exclusively according to the abstract concept described in Art. 348 CC, (…). On the contrary, the gradual appealing to social aims related to the use and exploitation of the different kinds of goods that the right of property may refer to has caused a diversification of the institution into a plurality of status endowed with different meanings and scopes.

22. *See* L. Díez-Picazo, *Fundamentos del Derecho Civil Patrimonial*, vol. III 56 (Cívitas 1995).
23. The expropriation is also studied *infra* Part III, Ch. 6, as a way of acquiring a right of property.

Therefore, courts and scholars generally admit the current 'plasticity' or 'flexibility' of property, which is shown through the existence of different types of property endowed with different legal status, according to the nature of the goods to which every property right refers.

43. Regardless of other categories such as intellectual property or property of goods belonging to the historical patrimony and declared to be of cultural interest, it is probably real estate, either urban land, forest and agrarian estates, or waters and mines, the one most intensively devoted to a social function. Owners of all these kinds of immovable things must accept that laws and plans (of administrative action) limit their powers, while at the same time they have to carry out positive and negative duties imposed by those same laws and plans.[24]

44. In conclusion, it is currently extremely difficult to find a leitmotiv that links the different kinds of property and permits to build a unitary concept of this right. Perhaps the sole connection point is what the CE calls the 'essential content' of the right, that is to say, the minimal elements necessary to make the right recognizable and that must be respected by the laws developing the constitutional provisions.

In the case of property, if the role of favouring personal dignity and individual freedom is required – and to recognize it as such – the lawmaker must respect the traditional using (*ius utendi*), renting (*ius fruendi*), and selling (*ius disponendi*) values of the goods. Nevertheless, the legal configuration of some kinds of objects, whose ownership is not endowed with one of these minimal elements, cannot always be qualified as unconstitutional. It is probably necessary to distinguish between private property as a generic institution in relation to which the essential content just described poses an impassable limit for the legislature, and the property in definite kinds of goods in relation to which the social function shows itself with stronger intensity. In the second case, the legislator has the competence to dig deeper than the essential content, provided that, if necessary, an expropriation process will be initiated.[25]

§2. The Concept of Ownership

I. Unity and Fragmentation

45. Despite the fact that ownership is not a unitary institution, – because it works in a very different way depending on the category of goods to which it refers – and although the bourgeois-liberal model of property must be currently considered superseded, taking the definition of *property* that is stated in Article 348 CC as a starting point, as well as describing the features of this right from a purely academic point of view, continues to be frequent with the goal of dogmatic exposition.

24. On this issue, *see infra* Part I, paras 95 et seq.
25. *See* L. Díez-Picazo, *Fundamentos del Derecho Civil Patrimonial*, vol. III 52–53 (Cívitas 1995).

46. Thus, ownership can be defined as a subjective right endowed with real efficacy and characterized as a result of its all-embracing content, which Article 348 CC describes using the terms *enjoying* and *disposing of* a thing.

The term *enjoying* refers to both the power to use (*ius utendi*) and the power to rent (*ius fruendi*) the thing that is owned. In other words, the owner not only has the power to use the object by himself/herself, obtaining from it a personal utility, but also to make all the fruits and products that the object is able to bear his/hers, whether because it is a fruit-bearing object by nature (e.g., agrarian terrain or cattle) or because it is a fruit-bearing object by means of a legal effect (e.g., money that bears interest, leasing a good in exchange for a certain price). Exercising the power to enjoy the object, the owner, unlike the holder of other real rights (e.g., the usufructuary), is not obliged to preserve the form and substance of the object; on the contrary, he/she may freely modify its shape, to the extent that he/she may even destroy it completely.

The term *disposing of* means the owner's power to alienate and encumber the object of ownership (*ius disponendi*). As for alienation, it must be understood that it applies to any title by means of which ownership is transferred from one person to another (e.g., sale, exchange, donation, or contribution of goods to a company), while encumbrance means the constitution of any (limited) real right in another's things, whether it is a right of enjoyment (e.g., usufruct or easement) or a right of guarantee (e.g., mortgage, pledge).

Making use of his/her power to dispose of the thing, the owner may also transfer it by means of inheritance, which distinguishes the property from other real rights that end as a result of the owner's death (e.g., usufruct). The owner may also voluntarily renounce his/her right, either in favour of a specific person, in which case the renunciation will normally be done onerously, or without the intention to favour any specific person, as occurs when a movable thing is abandoned by its owner, becoming a *res nullius*, liable to appropriation by anyone.[26]

47. Moreover, the owner of a thing is entitled to recover it from anyone who possesses or detains it without right and to obtain judgment, recognizing his/her ownership and ordering delivery of the thing to him/her. This action is explicitly mentioned in Article 348 CC.[27]

48. In accordance with the definition mentioned above, it is possible to talk about four basic features concerning the right of ownership:

(1) Abstraction. It means that ownership does not consist of addition of specific powers but comprises an indefinite number of powers. Actually it comprises all the possible uses and exploitations that the goods that are the object of property are able to have. As a result, it is almost impossible to fix its content with absolute accuracy. In contrast to property, the powers that the rest of real rights comprise can be defined accurately. To a certain extent, it could be said

26. On the appropriation, *see infra* Part III.
27. On the subject of this action, known in Spanish as *vindicatio* ('acción reivindicatoria'), *see infra* Part I, para. 92.

that the powers that the property include get actual entity only when they appear separated from the nucleus of the owner's right, forming the content of a limited real right.

(2) Elasticity. Property does not lose its essence although separated in several specific powers. Every one of them is included in the content of a limited real right. Property remains always as a sort of residual power, as a magnetic pole that attracts all the possible powers to itself when they stop being in another's hands. For example, when the usufruct ends, in the event of its holder's death, the powers to use and enjoy return to the bosom of the right of property.

(3) Perpetuity. Ownership tends to last as long as its object does, and not as long as its owner lives, that is to say, the length of a property right is marked by the physical or economic permanence of the object it falls upon, which permits it to differentiate ownership from certain limited real rights that have a life character. For that reason, the legal protection of property is closely connected with the legal protection for the right of inheritance (Article 33 CE).[28]

(4) Exclusivity. Every owner has the right to exclude any non-authorized action from another person that affects the goods that are the object of his/her property. Exclusivity also means that one right of property protected fully and simultaneously in favour of two different owners cannot exist, save in the case of co-ownership. However, none of the co-owners has a right to the whole object, but the property is equally divided into as many abstract quotas in the object as the number of co-owners.[29]

49. Although property is composed of an indeterminate number of powers, and despite the fact that the rest of real rights are known as 'limited real rights', it would be wrong to define *property* as an 'unlimited right'. The right of property, as any other subjective right, has limits. The term *limits* does not refer to the possibility that the owner constitutes one or more real rights upon the goods that are the object of property but to the existence of structural conditionings that modulate the exercise of that right by its holder with the aim of favouring general social interests or ones for other individuals.

The limits in favour of general social interests are justified by the widely known requirement that property fulfils a social function (*see supra*). Sometimes limits enable the owner to receive a pecuniary compensation, and sometimes this is not the case. Limits in favour of other individuals are connected with the prohibition of subjective rights being exercised in an exorbitant way (Article 7.2 CC): The owner may not act in any way that, without being beneficial to himself/herself, causes damage to another. Also he/she cannot forbid activities that are useful to other people but do not cause any damage to him/her (*ius usus innocui*). This doctrine has special application in the field of the so-called neighbouring relations, that is to say, the relations between owners of adjacent terrains or flats.[30]

28. Perpetuity is not present in the statutory treatment of some special kinds of property, such as intellectual property, which is subject to a legal length deadline.
29. On the co-ownership, *see infra* Part I, Ch. 5.
30. On this issue, *see infra* Part I, Ch. 6.

50. Ownership is the paradigm of real rights, but it is not the sole existing real right. Contrary to ownership, the other real rights are known as 'limited real rights' because its content consists of only a part of the utilities or exploitations that goods are able to offer. They are also called 'real rights in another's good' (*iura in re aliena*), thus they are always constituted upon goods that belong to another person.

A *numerus clausus* system functions in the Spanish legal order in order to 'create' real rights, which means that individuals may not constitute any limited real rights other than the ones that are typified by law. Limited real rights can be classified into two groups: on the one hand, the rights that give the holder some kind of power to use/enjoy someone else's goods and, on the other hand, the guarantee real rights that are constituted to assure the fulfilment of an obligation.

This second group of real rights gives the holder the power to demand the compulsory sale of another person's goods (the goods given as guarantee), as well as to apply the price so obtained in order to satisfy its right of credit.

51. In accordance with Article 333 CC, the goods liable to be the object of property and limited real rights are divided into movable and immovable ones.[31] The different legal status of these two categories can be observed in several aspects:

(1) The legal requirements both on capacity and power to alienation, that are needed to convey the property or any other real right, happen to be stricter when they refer to immovables than when they refer to movables (e.g., Article 323 CC).
(2) Putting a conveying contract into proper form in order to get the transfer and acquisition of property or any other real right in immovable goods (e.g., by means of donation; *see* Articles 632 and 633 CC), happens to be more complicated than doing the same with regard to a movable one.
(c) The system of legal publicity for real rights in immovables is more sophisticated than the one for movables because a public registry (called 'Land Registry') is organized for all kinds of immovables. As a result, who the owner of an estate is or who the holder is of whatever limited real right existing in an estate can be clearly determined, although in the field of movables, a public registry is foreseen only for certain categories of them, which makes possession emerging as the sole system of legal publicity for the remaining categories of movables. This does not mean that possession does not fulfil a function in the field of immovables as well, but it has a lesser significant function in this field.
(d) Lapse terms are shorter in the case of property and other real rights in movable goods. Moreover, in the scope of chattels, a smaller number of requirements are needed to enable an acquisition *a non domino* (*see infra* Part IV). In other words, in the scope of movables, there are not so many possibilities to bring a *vindicatio* successfully. The less intensity of the link between the

31. This is not the only possible classification for goods liable to be the object of property or other real rights, but it is the traditional one, as well as the most significant from a dogmatic point of view. Other classifications of the goods distinguish between corporeal and incorporeal ones; fungible and non-fungible ones; consumable and non-consumable ones; and private and public ones.

owner and the goods that are the object of ownership in the field of chattels is also proved by the fact that, in the case of seizure, chattels are distrained before immovable goods.

(e) Finally, it is worth mentioning that some limited real rights (e.g., easements) are liable to fall only upon real estate, although others are liable to fall only upon chattels (e.g., pledge), which clarifies the fact that the utilities vary depending on the type of goods concerned.

II. Immovable and Real Property (*See Also* Part I)

52. According to Article 334 CC, there are ten different kinds of immovable goods, although they are usually reduced, for didactic reasons, to four main categories:

(1) Immovable goods 'by nature' refer to tracts of land (Article 334.1 CC). Land is the only immovable defined in consideration of itself. Waters, mines, and quarries would also be included in this category (Article 334.8 CC).
(2) Immovable goods 'by means of incorporation' ('constituent parts'): the ones that are joined to other immovable goods in such a way that they cannot be separated without causing damage. This category includes trees, plantations, as well as buildings and every kind of construction or installation joined to the land in the form of stonework (Article 334.1, 2, 3, and 8 CC).
(3) Immovable goods 'by function' ('annexes'): all objects set within an immovable item by its owner in such a way that it shows the purpose of maintaining them permanently for the service of that immovable. Indeed they can be physically detached without causing damage from the immovable they belong to, which means that in this case the link mainly has an economic nature. Examples are ornamental objects, industrial machinery, agricultural fertilizers, and breeding places (Article 334.4, 5, 6, and 7 CC).
(4) Immovable goods 'by analogy': limited real rights that fall upon immovable things, as well as governmental grants to public works (Article 334.10 CC).

53. Traditionally, immovable goods, especially land and whatever is joined to it in a permanent way, have been characterized as a result of their greater economic value, given the agrarian character of the society. However, currently, with an economy based more on industrial and financial activities, chattels can reach a greater economic value than immovable goods within the individual's personal patrimony. It happens, however, that the land is not only rural land, liable to agricultural uses but also urban land, that has a huge value because of the strong demand for housing existing in our modern societies. In fact, it is not fortuitous that the so-called social function of property is applied basically to real estate, as said above. Several kinds of immovable goods, actually all of those so considered by nature, appear to be subject to a special legal regime of administrative laws, which intend to fix the extent of that social function for every one of them.

54. Although waters and mines are regulated through special administrative laws,[32] at this moment reference is made only to the administrative laws on urban land. In this respect, it must be said that the social function appears in the scope of urban property with such strong intensity that instead of a right with a typical content modulated by some limits, it is more suitable to describe it as an empty mould that can be gradually refilled at the same time as the owner fulfils the duties that the law requires at every stage of the development.

55. The legal regime on urban property is currently contained in the Legislative Decree 7/2015 on Land (recast text, 30 October 2015). This text defines the basic content of the right of property in land taking into account its social function, as well as setting the conditions for granting the essential equality in exercising that right in the whole national territory of Spain.

The State is not competent to legislate in matters concerning town planning, the CC AA being competent to design the legal treatment on urban land. But the state lawmaker, as STC 61/1997 (20 March 1997) stated, is competent to set basic conditions for granting the essential equality in exercising the right to urban property within every Autonomous Community, apart from its power to give other issues with influence over the statutory provisions on urban land, such as expropriation, land valuations, administrative procedure rules, and Public Administration's liability system.[33]

56. As seen below, the property on immovable goods is liable to detach itself, enabling many different limited real rights to fall upon it. Some of these rights allow, fully or partially, the use and enjoyment values of the goods – as is the case of usufruct, building and planting rights, leasing, emphyteusis, and the use and habitation or easements (*see infra* Part I). Others take advantage of the value of real estate as a guarantee, as occurs with a mortgage (*see infra* Part V).

III. Movable and Personal Property (*See Also* Part II)

57. The category of movable goods is defined in Article 335 CC by means of a simple contrast with regard to the catalogue of immovable things contained in Article 334 CC in such a way that all the rest of goods liable to be the object of property and not included in that catalogue must be considered chattels. Article 335 CC adds that, as a rule, movable goods are 'those ones that are liable to be moved from one place to another without damage of the immovable thing to which they were joined'.

Article 346 CC contains an interpretative rule on the use of the term *movables* in a contract or a legal provision. In accordance with this rule, the isolated use of the word *movables* must be understood as equivalent to movable things *stricto sensu*, that is, the pieces of furniture that serve as ornaments of the rooms. On the contrary,

32. The Law on Waters has been enacted in a renewed version on 20 Jul. 2001. As regards mines, the Law currently in force is Law 22/1973 (21 Jul. 1973).

33. For a more detailed study of property in urban land, *see infra* Part I, Ch. 2, §2. III.

the word *movables* used *lato sensu*, would also include money, jewellery, goods, securities, claims, books, weapons, medals, scientific or artistic collections, clothes, cars, grain, and liquid-good stuff, but this use must be clearly deduced by the context of the legal provision or contractual clause at issue.

Some incorporeal goods, that is to say, such as those that constitute the object of intellectual property rights (e.g., literary and artistic works, patents, industrial models, and patterns), are of a movable nature. Rights, obligations, and actions that apply to a movable thing are also incorporeal movables.

58. As said above, movable things have traditionally been considered those endowed with a lesser value within the individual's personal patrimony. This tendency has started to change in the last decades because it has been shown that some chattels have an equal or higher value than many immovable goods, which has currently allowed many loans to be granted on the basis of movable guarantees.[34] Therefore, the legal status of the most expensive movable goods (e.g., ships, airships, train wagons, motor vehicles, commercial establishments and intellectual property rights) is very close to that of the real estate – to the extent that a public registry, similar to the Land Registry, has been created with the aim of giving legal publicity to property and some other real rights in certain chattels.

First, contracts of leasing and sale on credit of non-consumable and identifiable movable goods are recorded in the 'Registry of Movable Goods', in such a way that the purchaser is subject to a legal 'prohibition of disposing' in order to guarantee the fulfilment of his/her obligation, and moreover, the seller, or the person who finances the deal, is authorized to introduce a 'reservation of title' – clause.[35] Second, the old 'Registry of Movable Mortgage and Pledge without Transfer of Possession', which had been operating since the enactment of the Law ruling both institutions in 1954, has been integrated into the Registry of Movable Goods.

In conclusion, it is possible to say that currently the legal regime of chattels is divided into chattels that are liable to publicity by means of registration, and chattels that are not.

59. The peculiarities of movable property will be analysed later, distinguishing between property in corporeal and in incorporeal chattels (*see infra* Part II). As regards limited real rights of enjoyment, none of them is actually exclusively applicable to chattels, as on the contrary so many of them are exclusively applicable to immovable goods (e.g., building and planting rights, emphyteusis, or easements), in such a way that the limited real rights of enjoyment applicable to chattels (e.g., usufruct, use) are also applicable to immovable goods. Consequently, giving a separated treatment to the rights of usufruct and use when falling upon movable goods is not considered necessary, but its exposition will be covered *infra* Part I, as well as the rest of limited real rights of enjoyment.

34. Concerning the classical real movable guarantees, such as 'movable mortgage' and 'pledge without transfer of possession', *see infra* Part V, Ch. 2.
35. On these two kinds of movable guarantees, *see also infra* Part V, Ch. 2.

60. It is however fitting to distinguish between the guarantee real rights in immovable goods (*see infra* Part V, Chapter 1) and in chattels (*see infra* Part V, Chapter 2). The movable guarantees, not only the ones mentioned *supra*, liable to be recorded in the Registry of Movable Goods, will be studied, but also others based on a merely possessory publicity, such as the pledge and the retention right.

§3. Estate and Patrimony

I. Unity and Fragmentation

61. As with any other expression of the principle of personal dignity and free development of personality, declared in Article 10 CE, every individual has the right to a patrimonial capacity, that is to say, a generic aptitude to be the holder of rights and duties with an economic content. The patrimony, first of all, assures individuals a minimal margin of freedom because it permits them to obtain by themselves the needed consumption goods and services. When an individual's patrimony is beyond its consumer needs, he/she is even able either to promote a private enterprise or to create a (altruistic) foundation.

62. From a different point of view, an individual's patrimony fulfils a function as guarantee with regard to the fulfilment of any legal obligation that his/her holder has incurred, in such a manner that in the case he/she does not pay a debt, the creditor may bring an action to obtain the seizure of all his/her goods, either present or future ones. This rule, known as 'principle of debtor's universal patrimonial liability', is stated in Article 1911 CC.

In the case of constitution of a guarantee real right, the debtor's liability would focus on one of the debtor's specific goods, which strengthens (and not excludes the application of) the principle of debtor's universal patrimonial liability.

63. Although *lato sensu* the term *patrimony* refers both to the rights that someone has to his/her credit and to the debts that are on his/her debit side, *stricto sensu* the term refers only to the assets that someone owns as well as to the rest of real rights that he/she holds. The fact of entire goods and rights belonging to the same person gives to that entirety a certain legal unity. So, for example, the Spanish CC refers to the patrimony of a person who is missing (Articles 181 and 187 CC) or to the patrimony of children subjected to *patria potestas* (Article 167 CC).

64. Despite the fact that an individual's patrimony can be considered as an entirety, there is no possibility of making a full transfer of it, at least not by means of a contract *inter vivos* so that one may not donate the whole of his/her patrimony because the law requires that the donor saves for himself/herself the goods needed to live according to his/her standard of living (Article 634 CC). Similarly, although it is possible to contribute to a company's patrimony with all the present assets (Article 1674 CC), the partner who makes such a contribution will maintain an abstract quota in the firm's patrimony. Therefore, the conveyance en bloc of an individual's patrimony may take place only *mortis causa*, through inheritance (*see infra* Part III, Chapter 3).

65. As a rule, a person may not create detached patrimonies; in other words, he/she may not divide his/her patrimony in such a way that some pieces of it remain immune to his/her creditors' hypothetical actions. Otherwise, the principle of debtor's universal patrimonial liability would be violated. Nevertheless, as an exception, it is allowed that certain masses of goods, liable to some definite categories of debts, be endowed with a relative legal autonomy.

66. This is the case of those spouses who decide to establish a marriage partnership (*see* Articles 1344 et seq. CC), that is to say, to make a common patrimony, basically composed of the profits derived from the work of both spouses, as well as of the fruits, rents, and interests borne by both the goods in the common patrimony and goods belonging to the particular patrimony of each spouse (Article 1347 CC).

The autonomy of the marriage patrimony with regard to the particular patrimony of each spouse is shown by the fact that, because of particular (unpaid) debts of each spouse, there cannot be automatically seized goods belonging to the marriage partnership (Article 1373 CC). At the same time, although particular goods of either of the spouses can be subject to the debts of the marriage partnership, the sums charged to the particular patrimony of one of the spouses will have to be reimbursed in a fitting proportion in the event of dissolution of the marriage partnership (Article 1398.3 CC).

67. The acceptance of an inheritance under the benefit of inventory should also be mentioned (Articles 1010 et seq. CC). The goods relating to an inheritance that has been accepted by an inheritor under the benefit of inventory are not combined with those belonging to that inheritor's particular patrimony, in such a manner that the inheritor that has accepted the inheritance under the benefit of inventory is obliged to answer for the debts of the inheritance only for the value of the goods belonging to the inheritance (liability *intra vires hereditatis*). When an inheritance, or a part of it, has been accepted by an inheritor under the benefit of inventory, a liquidation must be made with the aim of paying the debts of the inheritance. The inheritor at issue will receive only the remainder, if any exists. Due to this solution, the creditors of the inheritance cannot prosecute against the inheritor's particular patrimony.

When the inheritor does not accept the inheritance under the benefit of inventory, it is said that he/she makes a 'pure and simple' acceptance. In this case, the assets belonging to the inheritance are combined with the inheritor's particular goods, and consequently the inheritor may be obliged to answer for the debts of the inheritance with both the goods from the inheritance and his/her particular patrimony (liability *ultra vires hereditatis*). Despite everything, even in the case of pure and simple acceptance, the law intends to delay the effects arising from the combination of patrimonies following the division of the inheritance because the creditors of the inheritance may object to making such a division until their debts are paid or at least guaranteed (Article 1082 CC).

68. Currently, it is possible to create a single limited-liability company in Spanish Law, which permits a barrier to be built between the particular patrimony of the natural person who constitutes the company and the patrimony of the same person as sole partner of the company at issue.[36] Of course, in these cases, there will not be a detached mass of goods whose ownership corresponds to a unique natural person because the creation of a company, although a single one, gives rise to an artificial person endowed with a legal status clearly differentiated from that of the partner who created the company.

69. It must also be mentioned that individuals may destine part of their patrimony to constitute a foundation. The CE declares the right to create foundations as an expression of the right to private property (Article 34 CE).[37] Foundations may be created only for social interest purposes (e.g., cultural, scientific, educational, and sanitary), which impedes that they have the intention of benefit. After a foundation has been created and recorded in the Registry of Foundations, its patrimony is no longer a part of the founder's patrimony, but the patrimony of an autonomous legal entity.

70. Finally, since 2003, disabled people (or their parents or guardians if they are incapacitated) may create a separate patrimony in favour of their own needs. This patrimony, which must always be linked to that aim, will remain isolated from the rest of the holder's rights and assets, and it will be administered in accordance with a specific system of management and supervision. People other than the disabled and their parents or guardians may make contributions to this patrimony, even without the consent of the latter, provided that the contributor shows in front of the judge not only his/her interest but also that the contribution will be in the best interests of the disabled.

II. Trust and Fiduciary Mechanisms (*See Also* Parts IV and V)

71. It is possible to talk about 'patrimonial fragmentation' in yet another sense: when an individual appears as the owner of the entire goods that belong to him/her with a fiduciary character, that is to say, in such a manner that neither the property corresponds to him/her in order to satisfy his/her own interest (or at least not to satisfy it entirely) nor is the property conferred to him/her in order to satisfy his/her own interest as an authentic owner.

72. The fiduciary owner is part of a more complex legal relation, within which he/she has not the definitive interest as owner of the goods on which the trust falls. This does not mean that the fiduciary ownership does not give patrimonial advantage to the fiduciary owner because he/she can use and enjoy by himself/herself the goods at issue while the trust lasts, or he/she can use their value as guarantee, to assure himself/herself that another person (not the fiduciary owner) will pay a debt

36. On single limited-liability companies, *see* LSC (Legislative Decree 1/2010, 2 Jul. 2010).
37. The legal provisions for foundations are contained in Law 50/2002 (26 Dec. 2002).

contracted with the former. Therefore, the goods subject to any kind of fiduciary mechanism do not become integrated in a definitive way within the fiduciary owner's patrimony.

73. In Spanish Law, as occurs in most Civil Law countries, some fiduciary mechanisms with exceptional character are admitted basically in the field of Successory Law. Nevertheless, the trust is alien to our legal tradition and there are not any statutory rules on it. It is even said that the hypothetical admission of trust in Spain's legal system would be very difficult because it goes against several basic principles of the 'patrimonial Civil Law'.[38]

74. In Part IV, the fiduciary mechanisms conceived with a goal of management (*fiducia cum amico*) and the fiduciary mechanisms conceived with a goal of guarantee (*fiducia cum creditore*) will be studied in certain detail. Also, a distinction between *inter vivos* and *mortis causa* fiduciary mechanisms will be made.

§4. Possession and Title

75. Given the *erga omnes* efficacy of real rights, it is necessary that the role of holder of one of them can be known by anyone and not only by the contracting parties that have respectively conveyed and acquired the right at issue. In this sense, the acquisition of a real right by means of a contract (e.g., sale), even when put in writing, does not give enough legal publicity to the purchaser's right. The publicity of property and real rights is based on other kinds of acts, which permits one to state not only that someone acquired from another one a specific right on one specific date but also that the right at issue currently belongs to a specific individual.

76. The most sophisticated system of legal publicity for property and other real rights is the recording of them in a public Registry endowed with efficacy *inter privatos*. Such a system exists in Spanish Law, with general character, in order to get the registration – and therefore the publication – of property and other real rights in immovable goods. It is possible to do this through the 'Land Registry', whose way of operating will be basically described *infra* Part I, Chapter 2. For the registration of some real rights in some kinds of movable things, the Registry of Movable Goods has been foreseen (*see infra* Part II, Chapter 3).

77. Possession is the other method of legal publicity for real rights admitted by law. Possession can be defined as the exercise in fact of powers corresponding to a specific (real) right, from which the appearance of an authentic right arises. The law presumes that the person who possesses a right is the authentic holder of it. By means of possession, it is possible to make a provisional or presumable assignment of property and other rights in goods.

38. Such as the unitary conception of property, the *numerus clausus* system in order to 'create' real rights, or the principle of debtor's universal patrimonial liability. *See* J. de Arespacochaga, *El trust, la fiducia y figuras afines* 126–129 (Marcial Pons 2000).

78. The main effect of possession is the legitimation of the possessor, who will be able to act as the owner of the item possessed. In this sense, Article 448 CC presumes that every possession is based on an acquisition title, and it does not make it obligatory for the possessor to show his/her acquisition title: The person who brings an action against a possessor must prove that the latter does not have a valid acquisition title. Moreover, in the field of movable goods, the possessory legitimation causes beneficial effects to third parties.

The person who, in good faith, acquires movable goods from the hands of their possessor will be maintained at his/her position although it is subsequently proved that the transferor was not the authentic owner of the transferred goods (Article 464 CC). In other words, the risk of betrayal by the person who has been given the temporary tenancy of the goods by the authentic owner is for the owner and not for the purchaser, who may carry out an acquisition *a non domino*. The only exception to this consequence is when the authentic owner had been deprived of the item as a result of a theft or a similar illegal act.

79. Possession also fulfils other functions. For example, every possessor, due to the simple fact of possessing, has the power to demand a judicial protection against anyone who disturbs his/her possession (Article 446 CC). This protection is not subject to proof of an acquisition title but to proof of the simple fact that the plaintiff had previous possession of the goods or right at issue.

80. Possession is also shaped as a means to become the authentic owner of an object, in the case in which the possessor was not already the owner because of a failure in his/her acquisition title. This significant effect, known as acquisitive prescription (or usucapion), may take place in the course of time and, normally, provided the possessor is in good faith. On the acquisitive prescription as a way of acquisition of property and other real rights, *see infra* Part III.

Part I. Immovable Property and Real Property

Chapter 1. General Classification

81. As occurs in other Civil Law countries, Spanish Law ignores the distinction that one can find in Common Law countries between Real Property and Personal Property. Although it is true that this classification does not have any relationship with the kind of goods (movable or immovable) that are the object of the right, de facto is assignable to categories as immovable property and movable property, typical in Civil Law systems.

More exactly, given that Spain is a Civil Law country, one prefers the Roman category of 'real' rights (in the sense of 'rights in things'), which not only includes property but also limited rights (*iura in re aliena*).[39] The difference between these two concepts lies in the fact that property gives the owner the widest powers to use, enjoyment, modification and disposition over the object of the right, normally identifying the *right* with its *object* (often the term *property* or *properties* is associated with the object or objects themselves on which somebody's right of property falls). Otherwise, the so-called limited real rights, which are always compatible with the owner's right, do not give so wide powers for action.

Although property has a perpetual character (it is transferred to owner's heirs when the owner dies), *iura in re aliena* are generally submitted to a temporary limitation that is imposed by law (except contrary stipulation), normally coincident with the holder's life term.[40] Both property and limited real rights can indifferently fall upon realty or chattels, which shows clearly that what in Spain is called Real Property has a larger meaning than in Common Law countries. In fact, the expression *Personal Property* is widely unknown among Spanish scholars.

82. Property and limited real rights are the opposite category to claims or rights of credit (which are rights in personam). The main differences between them come both from their content and from the effects that they produce with regard to third parties (people who have not taken part in its constitution). Rights of credit are characterized by their relative efficacy because they may be asserted only against a specific subject – the debtor – who is held to carry out a definite performance in favour of the creditor and to whom the hypothetical action will be brought against in the

39. On this issue, *see supra* General Introduction, paras 34 and 50.
40. This limitation is intended to avoid indefinite burdens upon property.

case of violation of creditor's interest (*inter partes* efficacy). Real rights, however, give the holder a power of exploitation over a definite thing, which is opposable to any third party (*erga omnes* efficacy).

The CC classifies the rights of credit exclusively according to the kind of performance that the creditor may demand of the debtor (Article 1088 CC saying that 'any obligation consists in giving, doing or not doing (something)'). However, referring to real rights, the several types foreseen by the Law differ because of the number of powers given to the respective holder.

83. The set of rules for the major part of real rights is located in the CC, although the statutory provisions for some of them are contained in certain special laws, particularly for mortgage, whose legal treatment lies in the law related to the Land Registry (called, not very properly, 'Mortgage Law'), the right of exploitation in shifts of buildings for use by tourism, regulated in the homonymous law, or the building and planting rights, whose rules are included in laws on urban land and in the Land Registry Regulation.

84. Regarding limited real rights catalogue, scholars and courts discuss whether Spanish legal order follows a *numerus clausus* system (the only real rights are those typified by the law) or a *numerus apertus* one (private individuals may create their own new real rights, endowed with *erga omnes* efficacy). The conservative academic positions plead the first, alleging that this is preferable from the point of view of transactions' security. Contrarily, other authors opine that individuals are able to create new real rights, provided they intend to satisfy an actual and socially valid need and that they respect the characteristics of these kinds of rights.[41] The registrar in charge of the Land Registry, wherein immovable real rights must be recorded for them to have full *erga omnes* efficacy, is the authority who must carry out this control (*see infra* Chapter 2, §1).

85. There are also some important differences with regard to the origin of claims and real rights. Article 1089 CC says that 'obligations have their origin in law, contracts, quasi-contracts, and illicit acts or omissions'. Real rights such as property, usufruct and so on may also arise from law and contracts, but they may be acquired by means of successory mechanisms, accession, occupancy and usucapion as well (*see infra* Part III).

41. J.L. Lacruz Berdejo et al., *Elementos de Derecho Civil III. Derechos Reales*, vol. 2 10–12 (Dykinson 2009); L. Díez-Picazo & A. Gullón, *Sistema de Derecho Civil III. Derechos reales en general* 40–43 (Tecnos, 2016).

Chapter 2. Legal Interests

86. Unlike English Law, in Spanish legal order, the distinction between 'legal interests' and 'equitable interests' is totally unknown. In Spain, all rights (property and limited real rights) are – so to speak – 'legal interests', in the double sense that they have a statutory origin and that they have a general efficacy by which they result in being opposable to third parties.

However, it is noticeable that this general efficacy is in direct relationship with the role of Land Registry, whose object is to make real immovable rights known to third parties.

§1. Land Registry Function in Spanish Law

87. Land Registry, which appeared for the first time in Spain in 1861, is a public registry, coming into existence with the aim of providing security to juridical transactions. It gives publicity to titles in immovable goods, letting them be known to third parties – potential purchasers of the things/rights at issue. The rules on Land Registry and the basic principles of immovable property are contained in the Law on Land Registry (8 February 1946, with several subsequent reforms (LH)), as well as in its corresponding Regulation (14 February 1947, also frequently revised). Articles in the CC on Land Registry have little significance (Articles 605–608 CC).

88. Spanish Land Registry is an estates one, estates being taken as the basis whereon property or other titles acquired by them are recorded. This recording must be done by means of public documents,[42] wherein the creation, modification, declaration, alienation or extinction of these titles is noted (Article 3 LH).

Although the entry is neither obligatory nor constitutive of the rights, apart from exceptions like mortgage (Articles 1875 CC and 145 LH), recording gives many advantages in order to make the rights opposable to third parties.

89. The Spanish Law combines elements coming from two Registry systems, the French one and the German one, both of them thought to provide protection for third parties, purchasers of property or other real titles in immovable goods.

The French-model influence is clearly detectable in Article 32 LH, which says that 'property or other real titles in immovable goods not recorded in the Land Registry cannot be opposed against any third party', on the understanding that this 'third party' is any purchaser of property or other limited rights in an estate, who records his/her title, and additionally ignores the existence of any prior non-recorded right in the same estate. Therefore, the full efficacy of real rights in immovable goods requires not only their valid constitution but also their registration. A non-recorded real right in immovable goods cannot be asserted in front of the person who subsequently acquires, and records in good faith, a right of identical nature in the same immovables.

42. That is to say: notarial, judicial or administrative documents.

The German tendency can be appreciated in Article 34 LH, wherein the 'principle of protection for the appearance stemming from Registry entries' is stated. According to this article, 'the third party who acquires, by means of an onerous way, a right from someone, who in accordance with the registry entries appears with enough powers to transfer it, will be maintained in his/her acquisition, although the transferor's right is later declared null or rescinded because of reasons that are not stated in Registry entries'. This rule is conceived in order to protect a third party who, in good faith (i.e., to say, trusting in the Registry entries), has purchased the ownership of immovable goods, or other real rights in them, from the person who appeared as their holder in the Registry entries. The main effect of this rule is that the third party 'will be maintained in his/her acquisition', although subsequently the conveyor (holder in accordance with the Registry) may not be the actual holder of the transferred goods/rights. For this effect to be produced, the third party must (a) acquire by means of an onerous way; (b) be in good faith; (c) record his/her own right in the Land Registry, resulting in, in short, a *non domino* acquisition based on the aim of giving more security to juridical transactions with immovable goods.

§2. Immovable Property

I. Concept, Characters and Social Function

90. Article 348 CC defines property as the right to enjoy and dispose of an object without more limits than those set by the laws.

Despite the obvious significance that reaches the nature, movable or immovable, of the object on which the property falls, the Spanish CC does not categorically state different rules for movable and immovable property. It is true that some provisions refer exclusively to property in land (e.g., Articles 350 and 351 CC), but it answers rather to the agrarianism typical of the CC's age of publication than to the lawmaker's will of giving different rules for property in movable goods and property in immovable ones.

As the CC refers to the right of property *in genere*, except some special properties (such as intellectual property,[43] property on waters,[44] or joint ownership of blocks of flats[45]), authors frequently consider the *unicity* as a basic feature of property, together with other characteristics that make the property a right: *unlimited* (in the sense that it embraces the most extensive powers over an object), *perpetual* (opposite to usufruct – property does not last only for the holder's life), and *exclusive* (it is opposable *erga omnes*).[46]

43. 429 CC refers to the Law on Intellectual Property (enacted 12 Apr. 1996), in order to determine 'people to whom the right belongs, the way in which it may be exercised, as well as its duration'. For matters not foreseen in the special Law, general rules on property established in the CC will be applicable.
44. Its regulation is contained in Arts 407–425 CC, profoundly developed through the Law on Waters (20 Jul. 2001).
45. *See* 396 CC, which refers to Law 49/1960 (21 Jul. 1960), modified by Law 8/1999 (6 Apr. 1999). *See also infra* Ch. 6, §1, II.A.
46. On the general features of property, *see supra*, General Introduction, para. 48.

91. The right to private property reflected in our CC is characterized by a clear individualistic tendency, an obvious influence of the French Napoleonic Code. This individualism can be seen in the granting of absolute powers to the owner. This concept of property failed in the twentieth century, which opened the way for special statutes that began to take into account social needs as a criterion for defining the content of subjective rights, particularly property rights. An example of this is in the Law on Urban Leases (LAU) of 1946. This Law, passed with the aim of resolving the housing shortage after the Spanish Civil War (1936–1939), established a system of continuous compulsory prorogation in favour of lessees, which permits them to keep at will the enjoyment of the house to the detriment of lessors.

The CE of 1978, as has been said, embraces this new concept of property in Article 33, wherein, after declaring 'the right to private property and to inheritance', points out that 'the social function of these rights defines their content in accordance with the Constitution and the laws'. As our TC has indicated, the right enounced in Article 33 has two different aspects: the *individual* one, which gives its holder a set of powers over an object, and the *institutional* one, which imposes a bundle of duties and obligations, all of them according to laws, in view of collective values and interests, that is, the social function that every category of goods subject to property is called to fulfil.

II. The Defence of Property

92. Spanish legal order foresees several mechanisms of protection for property, but because of its significance, the *vindicatio* alluded to in Article 348 CC must be mentioned first.[47] It is a real action whereby a property title may be made out, brought by the owner (*dominus*) against the person in possession. *Vindicatio*'s aim is retrieving the object of property from the person who unlawfully possesses it.[48] The plaintiff must prove three points: (1) his/her own title; (2) the possession of the object by the defendant; and (3) the identity of the object to which the action refers.[49] Nevertheless, at least in the field of immovable goods, he/she is not obliged to prove that the object still belongs to him/her because ownership is presumed to continue in favour of the person who has proved its acquisition title.[50] This action must be exercised within a thirty-year term, starting from the day on which the dispossessed owner was able to exercise it.[51]

93. Besides the *vindicatio*, there are also other actions which can be carried out to obtain judicial protection for the right of property, as the 'declaratory' one, the

---

47. In Spanish, *acción reivindicatoria*.
48. *See* STS 30 Oct. 1997 (*RJA* 1997, 7344), STS 25 Jun. 1998 (*RJA* 1998, 4750) and STS 24 Jan. 2003 (*RJA* 2003, 611).
49. *See* STS, 3 Feb. 1996 (*RJA* 1996, 1084), 30 Oct. 1997 (*RJA* 1997, 7344) STS 25 Jun. 1998 (*RJA* 1998, 4750) and STS 8 Jul. 2011 (*RJA* 5010).
50. *See* STS 25 May 1946 (*RJA* 1946, 571) and STS 25 Mar. 1969 (*RJA* 1969, 1589). For movables, however, *see infra* Part II, para. 205.
51. Otherwise, the dispossessed owner could lose the property because of another's acquisitive prescription. On acquisitive prescription, *see infra* Part III, Ch. 3, §1.

'denial' one, and the action derived from a third party's property.[52] The first of these three actions is a real action, which can be exercised by the owner with the sole purpose of asking the judge to declare his/her property in a definite good.[53] The 'denial action' is one exercised by the owner with the double purpose of asking the judge both to declare that the ownership is free of any kind of charge or burden and to bring him/her back into the full enjoyment of his/her right.[54] Finally, the action derived from a third party's property aims to a declaratory judgment in favour of the plaintiff's ownership of a definite object, as well as to raise the seizure made in satisfaction of a debt, whose payment the plaintiff is not actually obliged to make (*see* Articles 595–604 LEC).[55]

94. Apart from these specific proceedings for the protection of the right of property, it is possible, under Spanish procedure rules, to bring a summary action in order to retrieve the lost possession of an object, provided that the plaintiff is able to prove that he/she has been in possession of that object before. These summary proceedings on possession are aimed only at restoring the factual situation in which the possessor found him or herself, thus forbidding violent acts of dispossession, even if coming from the actual owner. They do not serve to solve other issues, which must be clarified in the fitting declaratory judgment. Likewise, the summary possessory proceedings serve to protect everyone who possesses goods, whether his/her possession is based on a right that enables him/her to possess them or he/she possesses them unlawfully.

III. Urban Property

95. Urban property is one of the fields in which the distance between the current concept of property and the expansive conception of property coming from Roman Law can be observed more intensively because legal rules on urban land state in full detail the way in which every owner must exercise his/her powers (where, how, when and how much to build).[56] This legislative intervention is justified by the enormous economic significance of urban estates as the physical basis of productive activities and the key element for the implementation of the constitutional principle of family protection (Article 39 CE) and the right to a decent and adequate house (Article 47 CE).

96. In Spain, the first law on land (TRLS) was promulgated in 1956. Subsequently, several reforms followed each other, until the enactment of the urban land laws of 1976, 1992, 1998 and 2008. Currently, the statutory regulations of urban property are comprised in TRLS, approved by Legislative Royal decree 7/2015, and

52. The respective names in Spanish for these three actions are: *acción declarativa*, *acción negatoria* and *tercería de dominio*.
53. *See* STS 11 Oct. 1996 (*RJA* 1996, 7557) and STS 23 Mar. 2001 (*RJA* 2001, 4759).
54. *See* STS 27 Mar. 1995 (*RJA* 1995, 2325).
55. *See* STS 17 Dec. 2008 (*RJA* 2009, 292).
56. L. Díez-Picazo & A. Gullón, *Sistema de Derecho Civil III. Derechos reales en general* 151 (Tecnos 2016).

in Land laws enacted by CC AA in the exercise of their respective powers concerning 'territory ordination, urbanism and housing' (Article 148.1.3° CE).

The *ius aedificandi*, or power to build, inherent to the owner's right, is defined (e.g., positive duties to building or not building) in both land laws and urban development plans approved in every municipality. The latter's main functions are determining the land that must be preserved from the urban transformation (the so-called rural land) as well as the manner in which the development process must be carried out (e.g., types of building, height they should have).

97. The TRLS distinguishes three kinds of land: 'urbanized', 'rural' and 'land under an urban transformation process'. For every one of them, the TRLS confers a set of rights and duties on the respective owners.

98. The 'urbanized land' is the land from which you can have access to an urban set of infrastructures and services, already functioning, without the necessity of doing any transformations or works (except those which could provide the connection to all of these infrastructures) (Article 21 TRLS). Urbanized landowners have the right to build according to the requirements stated by applicable Laws and urban development plans and within a definite term.

99. 'Rural land' comprises, at least, three different kinds of land (Article 21.2 TRLS):

- The land that the urban development plans have classified as 'rural land' in order to fulfil the general rules – both from the TRLS of 2015 and from the Land laws enacted by the CC AA – that preserve certain lands from the urban development because of their specific values (historical, architectural, agrarian, forest, cattle, cynegetic or environmental values) or because of their values from the point of view of the landscape (e.g., National Parks).
- The land that the urban development plans have decided to classify as 'rural land' beyond the *minimum* stated by the Laws on Land (*see supra*).
- The so-called common rural land, which is the land that has not been considered as 'preserved' by the urban development plans (such as the latter two groups), but it does not have the main features to be classified as 'urbanized land' (i.e., it is not possible to have access from it to the ordinary urban infrastructures).

100. The 'rural land' should be assigned to an agrarian, cattle, forestal or cynegetic or other targets that imply a rational use of natural resources. Exceptionally, social and public interests may justify an urban development in this land.

101. Last, but not least, the TRLS mentions the 'land under an urban development process', that could take place either on an urbanized or on a rural land (in those exceptional cases, mentioned *supra*). In contrast to the static situation of the other two types, this land is affected by an urban transformation process that could consist either in the transformation of the rural land into an urbanized land – when the infrastructures and services are being carried out – or in the increase of the current infrastructures (Article 7 TRLS).

IV. Agrarian Property

102. Agrarian property is another field in which the transformation of property, through the incorporation of a social function, has intensely taken place. Articles 1 and 2 of the Law on Agrarian Reform and Development (1973 (LRDA)) contain the basic legal rules for rural property in Spain.[57] The first one points out, with emphasis, that the rural land must be used in the way that better corresponds to its nature, with subordination to community's needs. Likewise, Article 2 LRDA alludes to the fulfilment of a social function by rural estates.

The Modernization Agrarian Farming Law, approved in 1995, tries to adapt the agrarian legislation to the new needs of this market from a more opened position that takes into account other uses of the agrarian land (e.g., environmental protection and leisure activities). The Law makes easier the acquisition of the property on Rural Land by young people and foresees certain benefits for the people who do an agrarian activity as professionals.[58]

103. The rural property in Spain is characterized by the following features:

(a) In general, it is not liable to urban exploitation, but it must be assigned to agricultural, forestry, cattle, cynegetic or other targets linked to the rational use of natural resources.
(b) Owners of rural estates have the obligation of obtaining the best yield from the land. This duty is deduced not only from the LRDA but also from several laws of CC AA that sanction the agrarian and livestock infra utilization.[59]
(c) There are also contemplated tools meant to achieve the best exploitation of rural land for better exploitation. Particularly, the legal setting of the extension of the rural estates through the establishment of a 'farming minimum unit' – as a limit for the division of estates – that intend to cut short the problem of small properties stands out.

57. Some CC AA, exercising the competence given by the Constitution, have also enacted their own laws on agrarian property. Although Art. 149.1.23 CE gives to the State the exclusive competence for enacting laws on mountains, forest exploitations, and livestock roads, as well as on environment protection, this is a competence for enacting only the *basic* rules; that is to say, it does not impede CC AA to promulgate their own development laws.
58. This Law has been modified by Law 45/2007 (14 December).
59. On the incidence of (European) Common Agrarian Policy on these provisions since the date of integration of Spain into the EEC, *see* J.M. De la Cuesta Sáenz, *El Estatuto Jurídico del Suelo Agrario, Derecho Privado y Constitución*, No. 3 (1994), 131–168.

Chapter 3. Equitable Interests

104. This subject is not applicable in Spanish Law.

Chapter 4. Limited Interests

105. Contrary to ownership, limited real rights allow their holders to exercise only certain powers over other people's goods. Limited real rights' holders may obtain from the goods an exploitation always smaller than the one corresponding to owners. Limited real rights form a heterogeneous category, although all of them fulfil at the same time some common features. Thus, they attribute to its holder a direct and immediate power over the goods, or the holder's power is endowed with an *erga omnes* efficacy.

106. Depending on the type of powers that can be exercised over the goods, the *iura in re aliena* are classified as follows:

(a) Rights of enjoyment. They give the holder the power to use another's goods and, in certain cases, the power to enjoy them (e.g., taking the fruits that the goods produce). Within this category are included, among others, the rights of use and habitation, the right of usufruct and the easements.
(b) Guarantee rights. They allow the holder, creditor of a pecuniary amount, to urge the mandatory sale of the goods in which the guarantee lies, as well as to be paid with preference before other creditors with regard to the value obtained by this sale. The real guarantee rights may be opposed against anyone who happens to be the owner of the goods on which they fall.[60]

107. Taking into account its object, it is possible to distinguish three types of limited real rights. In the first place, there are rights that rest solely on immovable goods (e.g., easements). In the second place, some real rights may be held in only movable goods (e.g., the pledge). Finally, the rights that may indistinctly fall on movable and immovable goods (e.g., usufruct) must be mentioned.

108. Limited real rights receive special protection through what one could call the 'acknowledgement action',[61] which is the one that the holder of a limited real right may bring against the owner of the encumbered goods or against the holder of any other real right in the goods, when any of them do not recognize or diminish his/her right.

§1. USUFRUCT

I. Concept, Constitution and Statutory Provisions

109. Article 467 CC defines *usufruct* as the right to enjoy another person's goods with the duty of conserving its form and substance (*salva rerum substantian*). It is a right of enjoyment in another one's goods, which, contrary to property, is subdued

60. On this category of real rights, *see infra* Part V.
61. In Spanish, this action is known as *acción confesoria*.

to a temporal limitation: Normally it has a life character, extinguished by the usufructuary's death. Statutory provisions on usufruct are contained in Articles 467–522 CC. Several rules on special usufructs are included among them because of the object, such as rules on the usufruct of mountains (Article 485 CC), the usufruct of consumable goods (Article 482 CC), the usufruct of credits (Article 507 CC) and the usufruct of a whole patrimony (Article 506 CC).

The agreements or stipulations set by the parties are the first source of regulation, because, only in their absence, Articles 467–522 CC will be applicable (*see* Article 470 CC).

110. According to Article 468 CC, the right of usufruct can be purchased, without distinction being made between movable and immovable goods, by means of the law,[62] the will of individuals expressed through *inter vivos* or *mortis causa* acts,[63] and the acquisitive prescription.[64]

II. Subjects and Object

111. The holder of the right is the 'usufructuary', which may be either a natural person or a corporate body. When the usufruct is constituted in favour of a corporate body, it is subdued to a maximum deadline of thirty years, the aim being to preserve its temporal character (Article 515 CC).

The bare owner is the owner of the goods encumbered with the usufruct. The bare owner is legitimated to transfer and encumber its bare ownership (e.g., through the constitution of a mortgage or an easement), so as to carry out conservation acts and to make improvements or new plantations on the goods, provided that these activities do not reduce the usufruct's value nor damage, in any sense, the usufructuary's right. Among its duties, the payment of real burdens and taxes (Article 505 CC)[65] and the payment of extraordinary reparations (Article 501 CC) should be mentioned.[66]

112. With regard to the object, this right may fall on movable and immovable goods, a collection of goods (e.g., an inheritance), or quotas of co-ownership. A usufruct in rights, ex Article 469 CC, may also be possible, provided that they are neither inherent to person nor inalienable.[67] Although the most common case is the

62. In the CC, there is only an example of a right of usufruct directly originated by the law. It is the usufruct that corresponds to the widow or widower in a portion of her/his spouse's inheritance. This portion consists of a third of the inheritance if there are other inheritors of the deceased (Art. 834 CC) or a half if there are not (Art. 837 CC).
63. The most frequent case is the alienation of the bare property, with reservation of usufruct in the alienated thing.
64. On acquisitive prescription, *see infra* Part III, Ch. 3, § 1.
65. For example, taxes imposed on property (e.g., Patrimony Tax, or Tax on Immovable Assets).
66. Although the CC does not give a definition of these kind of reparations, it is possible to infer, from an interpretation a contrario of 500 CC, that these are reparations not caused by the ordinary use and are indispensable in order to preserve the thing in a good state.
67. An example of an inherent to person and inalienable right is the right to receive an alimony (Arts 142–153 CC).

usufruct in productive and non-consumable goods (Article 467 CC), the possibility of a usufruct in an object consumable by use is admitted expressly (Article 482 CC). In this case, the obligation of restitution that applies to the usufructuary at the deadline of its enjoyment will comprise the value assigned to the goods that are the object of usufruct. When the goods have not been valuated before the delivery, an equal quantity of the same kind and quality (*tantundem eiusdem generis*) – or its current price by the time when the right ends – shall be returned to the bare owner. The choice corresponds to the usufructuary.

III. Content

113. Unless an agreement has been made to the contrary, the usufructuary has a right to use (*ius utendi*) and a right to enjoy its fruits or profits (*ius fruendi*), either natural, or industrial or juridical in another one's goods (Article 471 CC).[68] On this issue, it is important to consult the Sentence of the Supreme Court (STS) 3 November 1988.[69]

The usufructuary also has the power to carry out improvements in the goods being the object of his/her right. These improvements may be removed at the end of the usufruct, provided that their removal does not cause damages or material injuries (*ius tollendi*).[70]

The usufruct is alienable by will of its holder (Article 480 CC),[71] who may also constitute a mortgage on it (Article 107 LH).

114. As regards the duties of the usufructuary, the CC imposes on him/her the obligation of making an inventory of the goods before starting to use them, as well as giving security that assures the fulfilment of his/her duties as holder of the right (Article 491 CC).[72] However, Article 493 CC allows the bare owner to excuse the usufructuary from these two duties.

While the usufruct is in force, the usufructuary is obliged to maintain the object diligently (Articles 467 and 497 CC),[73] and after the usufruct is extinguished, he/she must return the usufructed goods to the bare owner (Article 522 CC).

---

68. According to Art. 355 CC, 'natural fruits' are those that the land produces spontaneously, as well as offspring and other products resulting from animals; 'industrial fruits' are those that come from any kind of estate due to men's effort and cultivation; finally, 'civil fruits' or 'juridical fruits' are simply leasing rents or money interests.
69. *RJA* 1988, 8407.
70. *See* Art. 487 CC, which does not grant the usufructuary the right to be indemnified for making these improvements.
71. In accordance with this Article, the usufructuary also has the power to lease the usufructed good, provided that the lease ends when the usufruct is extinguished. There is a sole exception: the lease of a usufructed rural estate, which will subsist for the complete annual agrarian cycle.
72. These may not only be personal securities, as this Article strictly foresees, but also real securities, either in immovable (mortgage) or in movable goods (pledge).
73. Article 467 CC states the principle *salva rerum substantia*, i.e., the usufructuary's duty to preserve the shape and substance of the usufructed goods without changes. Art. 497 CC points out that, in the execution of this duty, the usufructuary must take care of the usufructed thing as 'a good paterfamilias'.

IV. Extinction and Liquidation

115. The usufruct ends when any of the causes mentioned in Article 513 CC occurs. These causes are the usufructuary's death, the termination of its duration term, the consolidation,[74] the renounce, the total loss of the object, the resolution of the bare owner's right, and the lapse.

After the right is extinguished, the goods that are the object of usufruct in question must be returned to the bare owner. However, Article 522 CC gives the usufructuary (and its inheritors) the possibility of keeping them in his/her power until the expenses made because of the usufruct, and whatever else that should be paid by the bare owner (e.g., expenses for extraordinary reparations), are reimbursed.[75]

§2. Building and Planting Rights

I. Concept

116. The right to build or plant on another one's land is called in Spanish Law the right of *superficie*. This right covers both the urban modality, which permits building on another's land, and the rural one, wherein the holder of the right (called *superficiario*) is legitimated to carry out plantations on another person's land.

The Spanish CC, contrary to the Italian and the Portuguese ones, does not contemplate a definition of this right, nor does it even dedicate a rule to design its basic legal scheme. Actually, the first to regulate this right in a certain detail has been the statutory provisions on land (*see* Articles 53–54 of the TRLS of 2015) and Land Registry (*see* Article 16 RH).

117. As regards its content, there is no unanimity among scholars to fix the powers it comprehends. From a traditional point of view,[76] it can be seen as a limited real right that entitles the holder to build or plant on another's land, subsequently acquiring the temporary ownership of the building or plantation, as an exception to the principle *superficies solo cedit* (*see* Article 358 CC). On the contrary, a modern interpretation says that it is purely the right to maintain the separated ownership of a building or plantation on someone else's land, which does not necessarily have to be constructed or planted by the holder.[77]

---

74. This is what occurs when the usufructuary becomes the bare owner of the thing (or vice versa) by means of a title (*inter vivos or mortis causa*) given after the usufruct has been constituted. The reason is that no one can be the holder of a limited real right in a thing whose property also belongs to him/her.
75. On the 'retention right', as a way of guaranteeing a right of credit, *see infra* Part V, Ch. 2, §3.
76. *See* L. Díez-Picazo & A. Gullón, *Sistema de Derecho Civil III. Derechos reales en particular* 46 (Tecnos 2016).
77. *See* R. Roca Sastre & L. Roca-Sastre Muncunill, *Derecho Hipotecario*, vol. V 475–476 (Barcelona 1997); I. De la Iglesia Monje, *El Derecho de Superficie. Aspectos Civiles y Registrales* 118 (Colegio de Registradores de la Propiedad 1996).

II. Urban Building Right

A. Concept, Statutory Provisions and General Features

118. It is a limited real right that entitles its holder to build on another one's land, obtaining the ownership of the resultant construction, or to maintain the separate ownership of a pre-existing building on another one's land.

Though, as has been pointed out before, the Spanish CC does not contain a systematic treatment for this right, this fact is not enough to qualify it as a non-typified right because some statutory provisions, both on land (Articles 53–54 of the TRLS of 2015) and on Land Registry (Article 16 RH)), refer to it.

From these statutory provisions, the following features derive:

(a) The urban building right must be recorded in the Land Registry as a requisite for its valid constitution.
(b) It is alienable.
(c) It is subject to a duration term.[78] At the time of its extinction, the owner of the land obtains the ownership of the building without having the duty to pay compensation.

B. Acquisition and Content

119. The urban building right may be purchased through either an *inter vivos* conveyance or a transfer by death. The legitimation to alienate it corresponds to the land's owner, or (when the right falls on a pre-existent building) to the building's owner. In the case of there being several owners, they all must give their consent because it involves a sort of disposal of the common goods (*see infra* Chapter 5). The owner is obliged to put the *superficiario* in possession of the land, as well as to allow him/her to build the construction.

120. The holder has the power to construct and maintain the constructed object on another person's land. He/she may alienate his/her right (*ius aedificandi*) in favour of third parties, as well as transfer or encumber the building. The holder has the duty to use the land, building on it (or maintaining the pre-existent building) in accordance with the purposes agreed, and to satisfy the agreed payment to the party that granted the right.

C. Extinction

121. Apart from general causes of extinction for real rights, the urban building right ends at the termination of the agreed duration term. It can also be extinguished by the rescission of the holder's title, due to the non-fulfilment of his/her duties.

78. 99 years. *See* Arts 53.2 LS 2015 and 16.1.a) RH.

The most important among the effects of the right's extinction is the reversion of the building into the hands of the land's owner. This effect is produced automatically, which means that the property is transferred *ipso iure*, without the need of a new purchase title or delivery, due to the principle of accession.

III. Rural Planting Right

122. The rural modality of *superficie* allows its owner to sow with seeds or plant crops on another's land, acquiring the ownership of the sown or planted.

The rural planting right may be constituted by the same means as for an urban building right. After purchase, the holder assumes the duty to sow or plant in the agreed conditions, as well as to satisfy the agreed payment. The land's owner is obliged to put the holder in possession of the land when the right is in force.

The rural planting right ends for the same reasons as those for the urban building right (the duration here is fifty years, unless otherwise agreed).

IV. Rights of Building Additional Floors and Sub-building

123. The construction of new floors in a building, or spaces under ground level, is a power inherent to the right of property in the building/land, which may however be split from it by the granting of a limited real right that entitles a person to carry out these activities on another's building or under another's land. These two rights, as happens with building and planting rights, involve an attributive effect with regard to the additional floors or the sub-buildings in favour of their respective holders.

Although the CC does not contain any mention of these two rights, the regulation on Land Registry refers to them (*see* Article 16.2 RH), on the occasion of setting the requirements for their registration. Among such requirements is the fixation of a participation quota included, which will be assigned to all of the new floors or sub-buildings within the building on/under which they are made.

§3. Leasehold Interests: Chattels Real (*See Also* Part II)

124. Holding immovable goods under lease implies the right to use someone else's immovable goods, for a definite period, in exchange for a certain price. Statutory provisions on leases are contained first in Articles 1542–1582 CC, devoted *in genere* to the lease of goods, either movable or immovable, so as in two special laws, one of them on urban leases (leases of buildings or flats, not necessarily meant for housing), and the other on rural leases (leases whose object is the agrarian, livestock or forestal exploitation of a rural estate). These are, respectively, the LAU, and the Law 49/2003 (26 November 2003), on Rural Leases (LAR).

125. Lease's nature is the object of controversy among scholars. Even though the lessee has a relationship of immediacy with the leased object, the lease gives the lessee a mere right of credit, which therefore has a plain *inter partes* efficacy. At least according to the CC rules, the leaseholder may not oppose his/her right in front of a third party. In this sense, Article 1571 CC allows the buyer of the leased object to finish the lease without the need to obtain the leaseholder's consent. However, the rule excludes the case in which another agreement has been made, as well as the provisions stated in the Law related to the Land Registry (LH). Indeed, Article 2.5 LH allows the registration in the Land Registry of immovable leases, to provide them with an efficacy opposable to third parties. After the lease is recorded, the subsequent purchaser of the estate may not finish it. On the contrary the purchaser is obliged to maintain the lessee's use of the object until the end of the lease.

Apart from this, the LAU used to declare the opposability *erga omnes* of the lease assigned to housing, for a minimum period of five years, before every subsequent purchaser of the leased house, even though the lessee's right had not been recorded. However this rule has been changed by means of the Law 4/2013 (4 June 2013), which modifies the LAU (*vid. Infra*). Currently, the urban lease must have been registered if the holder wants his/her right to be opposable against a third party. On the contrary, the LAR states that the purchaser of the estate is obliged to subrogate the lessor, regardless of the registration of the right in the Land Registry (Article 22 LAR).

126. The lease contract is a bilateral and onerous one. The general principle of freedom of form applies to this contract (Article 1278 CC).

When the contract concerns urban-built estates, the rules contained in the LAU are applicable.[79] If the lease rests on rural estates, one has to look for its rules in the LAR. In both cases, the rules on leases contained in the CC (Articles 1542–1582 CC) are applied only with a supplementary character, regardless of the fact that they are the main statutory provisions for leases in movable goods and leases in urban, non-built estates.

I. Urban Leases

A. *Special Statutory Provisions*

127. The first LAU was enacted in Spain in 1946. It was followed by a second Law in 1956, the LAU passed in 1964, the important reform of the latter made in 1985, and finally the law currently in force: the LAU, which applies only to contracts signed after its coming into force This Law has been widely modified by Law 4/2013 (4 June 2013) aimed to provide more flexibility to the lease market by means of recognizing the two parts of the contract the right to regulate their contractual relationship without most of the limits of the prior legislation.

The appearance of special laws on urban leases is linked in Spain to the scarcity of housing and the increase of immovable speculation that followed the civil war

79. Nevertheless, the LAU is not applicable, among others, to military and university housing and housing given to employees because of their jobs, all of them regulated by their respective statutory provisions.

(1936–1939), circumstances that made necessary the adoption of a series of measures aimed to protect housing leaseholders. Among these measures, the mandatory prorogation of the contract without limit of time gained importance, which guaranteed the leaseholder permanent use of the housing for his/her entire life by means of the successive and automatic prorogation of the contract: Only the lessee was entitled to finish the relation, being obliged to notify the lessor of his/her decision within the corresponding term.[80] Although this rule was removed in the reform of 1985, it is still applicable to many leases made before 9 May 1985.[81]

128. The current LAU provides two different categories of leases. First, housing leases, which have as object a habitable building whose primary function is the fulfilment of the lessee's need for permanent housing. Second, the so-called leases for any use other than housing, wherein seasonal leases of urban estates,[82] together with leases aimed to undertake an industrial, commercial, professional, cultural or teaching activity in the building, are included.

Only with regard to the first category of leases, the LAU grants leaseholders a series of prerogatives, although many of them have been removed by the recent modification introduced by Law 4/2013, as we will *see Infra*. Among them it is worth mentioning the right to get the annual renewal of the lease by the sole will of the lessee, until the completion of a minimum period of three years (five before the modification of Article 9 by Law 4/2013), provided that the lease had been agreed upon for a shorter period of time. The leases for a use other than housing are regulated mainly by the parties' arrangements. If these arrangements are lacking, the few rules that the LAU dedicates to this kind of leases are applicable, as are the CC rules, although with a supplementary character.

B. *Content of the Right*

129. The lessee has the right to use the leased building, but he/she must use it according to the aim for which the lease has been agreed. Coherent to this duty, the LAU foresees the carrying out in the housing of annoying, unhealthy, harmful, dangerous or illicit activities (Article 27.2.f LAU) as causes for the rescission on lessor's demand.[83]

Among the duties applicable to the lessee can also be mentioned the duty of paying a pecuniary compensation to the lessor (i.e., technically called 'rent'), which must be satisfied within the first seven days of every month unless the agreement states otherwise. In leases concerning housing, the advance payment of more than one monthly instalment (Article 17.2 LAU) may not be required.

80. Even after the lessee's death, two successive and compulsory subrogations in favour of the inheritors were foreseen.
81. *See infra* para. 134.
82. According to the jurisprudence, this category includes 'those leases characterized by a seasonal, circumstantial and non-permanence vocation'. *See* STS 26 Mar. 1997 (*RJA* 1997, 2538).
83. STS 4 May 1999 (*RJA* 1999, 2880) considered annoying the settlement of a disco that emitted sounds with strong intensity.

The lessee is obliged to maintain the leased building and to give it back to the lessor at the end of the contract in the state in which he/she had received it. The LAU states that the lessee is responsible for the damages caused in the building by his/her fault or by the fault of people living in the house (Article 21 LAU).

Maintenance necessary for the house to be used in accordance with the agreement must be paid by the lessor (Articles 21 and 30 LAU). On the contrary, small reparations derived from the deterioration caused by ordinary use are the lessee's responsibility. Article 23 LAU allows the lessee to make improvements, although two limitations are stipulated: These works cannot modify the building's configuration or its accessories nor diminish its stability or security.

Finally, the lessee has a preferring acquisition right in the case of alienation of the leased estate, unless otherwise agreed (Articles 25 and 31 LAU).

C. The Mandatory Prorogation of the Housing Lease

130. The LAU allows the parties to freely arrange the lease's length. However, for leases having as object a building aimed for housing agreed upon for a period shorter than three years, the successive prorogation of the contract for annual periods until the three-year minimum term is achieved has been provided (Article 9 LAU). This prorogation is automatically applied unless the lessee expresses to the contrary within the thirty days prior to the expiration of the contract. This automatic effect may be neutralized in case of lessor's need of housing, or even his/hers close family's (first grade relatives, by consanguinity or adoption) or ex-husband's or ex-wife's in case of separation, divorce or marriage nullity (once there is a final judgment). In all these cases, the lessor is obliged to notify the lessee his/their need of housing within the term of two months in advance, provided that the lease had last at least a year (first year of duration of the contract).[84] Before the modification introduced by the Law 4/2013 (4 June 2013), the LAU granted the leaseholder special protection during the old five-year minimum period. Thus, the lessor could not increase the rent during this period on the basis of improvements made in the leased house (Article 19 LAU) nor update the rent unless according to the extent of the variation expressed by the Official Index of Consumer Prices (the so-called IPC). Moreover, in the case of alienation of the house, the lease was opposable to the buyer, who was obliged to subrogate the lessor for the time until the end of the contract (included eventual prorogations). This effect did not depend on the registration of the lease in the Land Registry (Article 14 LAU). According to the current Law, many of the measures of protection to the leaseholder have been removed in order to encourage property owners to enter into lease agreements to satisfy the growing demand for housing in Spain. First, the rent may be increased now during the whole

84. In order to avoid possible frauds, Art. 9.3 LAU foresees that, if within three months after the extinction of the contract, the lessor (or his/her spouse or relatives) had not occupied the housing by himself/herself, the lessee will have the right to return to the housing for a new period of three years and to be indemnified because of the expenses resulting from vacating the house. The lessee has, as a choice, the power to demand from the lessor a compensation equivalent to a monthly rent for every remaining year until the end of the three-year period.

term of the contract without the need of submitting its revision to any Official Index. However, the prohibition for the lessor to increase the rent on the basis of improvements made in the leased house is still in force, but only during the three first years of the contract. And last, in case of alienation of the house, the lease will be opposable to the buyer (with the subsequent subrogation of him/her in the contract instead of the lessor) only when it has been recorded in the Land Registry, like the rest of rights upon immovable goods (property or limited real rights) (new Article 14 LAU).

131. Apart from the mandatory prorogation, when the leaseholder has kept the house beyond the three-year term, the lease may continue due to a 'tacit renewal'. In accordance with Article 10 LAU, if the three-year period has passed and none of the parties has notified the other, at least one month in advance, of his/her other intention, the contract will be renewed for one more year, compulsorily for the lessor and voluntarily for the lessee.

D. Registration

132. As said above, the statutory provisions on Land Registry (*see* Article 2.5 LH) allows registering leases on immovable goods, with the aim of granting them a general efficacy, that is, such an efficacy to make them opposable to third parties (e.g., buyers of the leased estate).

In this field of the registration of the leases, one of the most important modifications of the LAU has been carried out by means of the Law 4/2013 (4 June 2013). Before June 2013, the Law provided the opposability *erga omnes* of the right, whether it had been registered or not, but only for a five-year period (Article 14 LAU). In the case in which the lease had been registered in the Land Registry, it would be opposable for the whole duration of the contract, even longer than five years, before the subsequent purchaser of the estate (Article 14 LAU). But, now, the opposability *erga omnes* of the right depends exclusively on its recording in the Land Registry. In other words, if the leaseholder did not get to record his/her right in that Registry, his right will not be opposable to the buyer of the leased estate (who could decide freely if he/she subrogates the lessor or not) or to the holders of whatever real rights have been constituted upon it.

E. Extinction

133. The lease is extinguished as a result of the rescission either on lessor's or on lessee's demand, based on the non-fulfilment of legal duties or contractual arrangements. The extinction of the lease is also foreseen due to the termination of the arranged period; the destruction of the leased building not caused by the lessor; and the statement of imminent collapse provided by the competent authority (Articles 27 and 28 LAU).

F. Transitory Period

134. Under the rules on urban leases prior to 1985, the right of a housing leaseholder had a for-life character by virtue of the mandatory prorogation system described above. This mechanism for the protection of housing leaseholders was suppressed by the legal reform passed in 1985. However, until now, every contract signed before 9 May 1985, the date when the reform came into force, continues to be subject to statutory provisions corresponding either to the LAU enacted in 1964 or even to previous laws. Therefore the mandatory prorogation is still applicable to many housing leases.

Despite everything, some rules in the current LAU have been included related to leases purchased before the 1985 reform. These rules are aimed at reducing the two main effects linked to the mandatory and successive prorogation: the rent freeze and the *mortis causa* subrogation in favour of certain relatives after the death of the lessee. The current LAU has introduced a mechanism for bringing up to date antique rents, at the same time that it has limited the total number of possible *mortis causa* subrogation in the lessee's contractual position.

With regard to the last important modification of the LAU by the Law 4/2013 (4 June 2013), the new regulation will not be applicable to the lease contracts concluded before it.

II. Rural Leases

A. Special Statutory Provisions

135. The main cause that forced the appearance of a special statute on rural leases was, as in the case of urban leases, the desire to grant leaseholders better protection.

The first Law on the matter was the LAR, passed in 1935, although law currently in force is LAR, which has been modified in 2005 and 2015 relating to the duration, the contract formalities, the rent and the improvements of the estate made by the lessee. Several laws enacted by some CC AA in the exercise of their powers must be added as well. Accordingly, the rules on leases in the CC fulfil a mere supplementary role.

B. Content of the Right

136. The right of rural lease entitles its holder to obtain a definite agrarian, livestock or forestry exploitation from another's estate in exchange for a price or rent. More precisely the leaseholder is entitled 'to use the estate according to the aim for which it has been leased'. This limitation does not impede the lessee from changing the crop being grown, but he/she must return the land to the lessor at the end of the contract 'in the same conditions as received' (Article 8 LAR). Therefore, the lessee is responsible for the damages caused to the leased estate by his/her fault or by the fault of people working under his/her dependence. In accordance with the right to use and enjoyment, the lessee is obliged to pay the lessor a price (the 'rent'), which in principle must be agreed in money, although a payment in kind is also possible (Article 13.1 LAR). The payment of the rent will be made annually, though the payment of a unique amount for the whole extent of the lease may also be fixed (Article 13.3 LAR).

Necessary maintenance or reparations are lessor's responsibility ex 18 Article LAR. However, the lessee is allowed to make improvements according to Articles 20–21 LAR.

C. The Mandatory Prorogation of the Rural Lease

137. The LAR fixes a mandatory five-year minimum period for rural leases, with the aim of guaranteeing the leaseholder enough stability to get some benefits from the exploitation of the land. After the lease finishes, the LAR foresees a voluntary prorogation for a new five-year period if the lessor does not notify the other party his/her intention of retrieving the estate a year before the contractual term finishes, nor the lessee brings it back to the lessor at the end of the contract.

D. Registration

138. Even though rural leases may be registered in the Land Registry according to the Article 2.5 LH, which provides for the registration of immovable leases, Article 22 LAR states its opposability against the estate's purchaser, who will have to subrogate the lessor, whether the registration has been made or not.

E. Extinction

139. The right of rural lease is extinguished as a result of any of the following causes: (a) rescission of the contract, at the request of any one of the contracting parties, based on the non-fulfilment of the duties corresponding to each one; (b) total or partial destruction of the estate if not the fault of any one of them; (c) termination of the arranged period or its prorogations.

§4. Emphyteusis and Rent Charge

I. Ground Rents: Concept and Classes: The Emphyteusis

140. Ground rents, which currently have little space in the Spanish social reality, can be assimilated to what Article 1604 of the Spanish CC calls *censos*. According to this provision a ground rent comes into existence when 'some immovable goods are kept subject to the payment of an annual allowance or pension in exchange for the total or partial ownership of these goods, or in exchange for a capital received in cash'. Thus, this is another real right in another one's immovable goods, in such a manner that the holder of the right may demand the payment of an annual pension from the land's owner subject to the burden on which the ground rent consists. The encumbered estate guarantees the fulfilment of this duty, for which the holder may request its mandatory sale to collect the overdue pensions with the price so obtained (Article 1623 CC).

The CC distinguishes three types of ground rents: one constituted by consignment, one constituted by reserve and the emphyteutic one. The first one is defined in Article 1606 CC as the ground rent constituted by a person in an immovable belonging to him/her, in exchange for a capital that he/she receives in cash from another person, in such a way that the former acquires the duty to pay the latter a periodical allowance. In the ground rent constituted by reserve, somebody purchases from another the ownership of an immovable, with the obligation to pay the transferor a pension guaranteed by the purchased good (Article 1607 CC). Finally, the emphyteusis is relevant when an individual gives another (the 'emphyteuta') the so-called useful ownership of an estate, keeping for himself the so-called direct ownership, in exchange for an annual pension.

Therefore, in the emphyteusis, the 'direct owner' is empowered to receive a pension, which could be an amount of either money or in kind. On his/her side, the emphyteuta has the right to acquire all the products and accessions of the land (Article 1632 CC). The emphyteuta may transfer his/her right to third parties through *inter vivos* or *mortis causa* acts, which will not affect the direct owner's right (Article 1633 CC). If, at the moment of the emphyteuta's death, there were no inheritors, the direct owner will recover the full ownership of the estate (Article 1653 CC).

II. Constitution and Characters

141. Ground rents may basically be constituted by means of contract, testament or usucapion.

These rights have perpetual or, at least, undefined character (Article 1608 CC), although it is possible to define a definite length, and, except stipulation to the opposite, the contracting party obliged to pay the allowance may extinguish the ground rent by 'redemption', through payment to the holder of an amount of money.

Ground rents are alienable *inter vivos*, both onerously and gratuitously (Article 1617 CC).

III. Extinction

142. Among the causes of extinction of ground rents, the following must be mentioned:

(a) The redemption, which consists of the payment of an amount of money by the contracting party obliged to pay the allowance to the holder (*see* Articles 1651 and 1662 CC). Nevertheless, by mutual agreement, it is possible to forbid the

redemption for a certain number of years, as well as for the life of either the first holder or another defined person (Article 1608 CC).
(b) Total destruction of the estate.
(c) Total expropriation of the estate. Related to the emphyteusis, the specific rule of Article 1631 CC must be considered, which says that in the case of partial expropriation the right may subsist for the remaining part of the estate.

§5. Use and Habitation/Occupation

I. Concept, Statutory Provisions and General Features

143. The rights of use and habitation are the object of legal treatment in Articles 523 and 529 CC, although these statutory provisions will apply only if there are no other agreements signed between the parties.

Some CC rules on usufruct, are also applicable, for example, those that obligate to make an inventory (Article 491 CC) or to take care of the goods as a 'good paterfamilias' (Article 497 CC), provided that they are not in contradiction with the rules given specifically on use and habitation (Article 528 CC).

144. The right of use, according to Article 524 CC, 'gives the power to receive an amount from the whole fruits produced by another one's goods, enough to satisfy the needs of the holder ("user") and his/her family, even when the latter increases'.

As the rule says, the right of use legitimates the holder to obtain the fruits from someone else's goods, but to such an extent to be much more limited than the one corresponding to a usufructuary, because its goal is only to meet the needs of the user and his/her family. After these needs have been satisfied, the user is obliged to return the surplus to the owner, under the penalty of abuse, specifically considered in Article 529 CC as a cause for the extinction of the right.

Even though the rule does not indicate it, the use allows the user to possess the goods and not only to demand the obtained fruits from the owner. Nevertheless, if the holder had a right to receive only a part of the fruits, then the possession must be shared with the owner of the goods.

Among scholars, there is controversy about the meaning that, in this context, must be given to the term *family*. Some authors maintain a wide interpretation, according to which the holder has a duty of alimony to include all the people related to him/her, although they do not reside in the family house.[85] On the contrary, other authors limit the application of this rule to the relatives that reside with the user and are linked to him/her by consanguinity ties.[86]

85. Articles 142–153 CC contain the rules on the legal duty to pay alimony to some relatives in the case of need. The alimony must cover the costs of sustenance, housing, clothes, and medical assistance. This duty concerns spouses, ancestors, descendants, and also partially-related brothers and sisters.
86. I J.A. Doral García, *Comentario de los Arts 523 a 529 CC, in Comentarios al Código Civil y Compilaciones Forales* 481 (M. Albaladejo & S. Díaz Alabart, Tomo VII, eds., Revista de Derecho Privado 1980).

145. As regards the right of habitation, Article 524.II CC describes it as a right that empowers its holder to occupy, in another person's house, the rooms necessary for him/her and the members of his/her family. Contrary to the right of use, habitation can lie only in habitable buildings.

146. The rights of use and habitation are *iura in re aliena*, belonging to the category of the rights of enjoyment. Both of them have a for-life character. Some scholars understand that particularly the right of use is a sort of limited usufruct.[87] Other authors defend the entire autonomy between both figures.[88] The inalienable nature of the rights of use and habitation favours the latter thesis, which is justified by its inherence to the holder,[89] contrary to the free and full alienability that characterizes the right of usufruct.

147. Related to the powers and duties of the parties, it is worth mentioning Article 527 CC, which fixes the extent in which the holder of any of these rights must contribute to the ordinary expenses made for the maintenance of the object in question, depending on the extension of his/her right.

II. Constitution and Extinction

148. The CC does not mention the methods of constitution for the rights of use and habitation. Lacking a voiced provision, academicians normally point out three different methods: the law itself, an *inter vivos* or *mortis causa* alienation and usucapion.

149. Article 529 CC indicates that the rights of use and habitation are extinguished by the same causes as usufruct and also by severe abuse of the used or occupied object. There is a clear difference with regard to usufruct at this point because Article 520 CC provides that the usufruct is not extinguished by misuse of the goods that are the object of the right.

§6. Easements and Profits

I. Concept, Classes and Features

150. Easements are regulated in Articles 530–604 CC. They are limited real rights of immovable character constituted in someone else's estate (the so-called

87. L. Díez-Picazo & A. Gullón, *Sistema de Derecho Civil III. Derecho de Cosas y Derecho Inmobiliario Registral* 432 (Tecnos 1998).
88. I J.A. Doral García, *Comentario de los Arts 523 a 529 CC, in Comentarios al Código Civil y Compilaciones Forales* 481 (M. Albaladejo & S. Díaz Alabart, Tomo VII, eds., Revista de Derecho Privado 1980).
89. 525 CC indicates that 'the rights of use and occupation may not be leased or alienated to another person by means of any title'. 108 LH forbids that either of these two rights constitutes the object of a mortgage.

servient estate) for the advantage of two or more persons or for the benefit of another estate belonging to a different owner (the so-called dominant estate). In the first case, one speaks of 'personal easements' and, in the second one, of 'estate easements'.

In Spanish Law, easements can be positive or negative. The first ones, which will be analysed in this section, allow the holder of the dominant estate to use the servient estate in some way (e.g., passing through it on foot or by car, pumping water from it, or allowing water to pass through it). 'Negative easements', which forbid the owner of the servient estate to do something that will be licit for him/her to do if the easement did not exist, will be studied *infra* §8, under the epigraph 'restrictive covenants'.

151. Articles 549–593 CC contain detailed provisions on a series of easements, which can be characterized as 'typified easements'. Actually, many of them cannot be considered genuine easements – given the lack of service or utility relationship between two estates – but rather generic limits to the right of property imposed by the law with the goal of guaranteeing neighbourly relations.[90] Therefore, it must be considered a systematic deficiency that the CC employs, in some of the cases, the word *easement*.

As regards the real easements,[91] these should be described as mandatory easements, in the sense that the law gives a person the power to demand from another person its constitution. According to this scheme, the easement may be purchased through a juridical act agreed upon between the affected owners, or through a decision from the judicial authority, when the owner of the servient estate does not consent to the easement.

Apart from the typified easements, private individuals may constitute as many easements as they want, provided that they do not infringe upon the law or the public order (Article 594 CC). These non-typified easements are called by the CC 'voluntary easements'.

152. The basic features of positive easements are as follows:

(a) It is required that the two estates affected ('dominant estate' and 'servient estate') belong to different owners.[92]
(b) They are inseparable from the estate to which they belong (Article 534 CC), which means that they may not be transferred or mortgaged separately from the dominant estate.
(c) They consist of a utility that the servient estate gives to the dominant estate (in the case of estate easements) or to the person or persons who are the easement's beneficiaries (in the case of personal easements). This utility can be either agrarian (e.g., transit through the servient estate(s) for farming and harvesting in

90. On this issue, *see infra* Ch. 7.
91. Among them could be mentioned the right-of-aqueduct (Art. 557 CC) and the right-of-way (Art. 564 CC).
92. With regard to this requirement, *see* STS 3 Jan. 1992 (*RJA* 1992, 146).

favour of an estate enclosed among others),[93] urban (e.g., easement that allows its holder to move materials through the estate of another person, to set a scaffolding or other installation on it, to build a construction or to make repairs to a building situated on the dominant estate),[94] or industrial (e.g., the passing of telephone wires or pipelines). The utility must come directly from the estate, and not from the work carried out by a person.

(d) Unlike other real rights, easements are perpetual, unless agreed otherwise.

II. Subjects and Object

153. Two people are tied by the relationship created with the easement: the easement's holder and the owner of the servient estate. In the case of estate easements, the holder of the right is the owner of the dominant estate.

The owner of the estate that is going to be burdened is legitimated to constitute the easement (Article 594 CC). If there are several owners affected, all of them must give their consent (Article 597 CC).

Easements can lie only in estates, or in a part of one of them.

III. Constitution

154. Possible ways of constitution for easements are as follows: the law, the 'autonomy of will' (contract, testament and similar juridical acts), the acquisitive prescription and the so-called constitution by apparent sign.

155. As regards law, it has already been said that, when the CC refers to 'legal easements', in some cases, they are merely generic limits to the property, and in the rest, there is not automatically a right created but a person empowered to demand from another the mandatory granting of the easement. There will be necessarily either the achievement of an arrangement or in the event of non-agreement, the intervention of a judge.

156. As regards the autonomy of will, all type of juridical acts are admitted, onerous or gratuitous, *inter vivos* or *mortis causa*, Article 594 CC providing a wide margin for private individuals in this field.

157. Some special rules on the acquisitive prescription of easements are foreseen in Articles 537–540 CC. What these rules do not provide for must be supplemented with the general rules on acquisitive prescription.[95]

158. Finally, the possibility of purchasing an easement 'by apparent sign' must be mentioned. This modality is also known as constitution 'because of destiny

93. *See* Art. 564.III CC.
94. *See* Art. 569 CC.
95. *See* Arts 1940–1960 CC. *See also infra* Part III, Ch. 3, §1.

assigned by the paterfamilias' or simply 'tacit constitution' (Article 541 CC). In accordance with this rule and with jurisprudence,[96] the requirements for an easement to be constituted in this way are as follows:

(a) The existence of an external sign that shows a service relationship between two estates, or two parts of an estate, belonging to the same owner (e.g., a path that facilitates the passing through of one of them for the benefit of the other).[97]
(b) The establishment of the sign by the owner of the estate(s).[98]
(c) The maintenance of the sign after the alienation of one of the estates (or parts). The sign may be factually eliminated before the granting of the title of property or may be eliminated by express statement included in the alienation title.[99]

IV. Content of the Right

159. Fixing the content of this right requires paying attention first to the arrangements provided by the parties (Article 598 CC). If these arrangements are not made, the rules in the CC will be applicable (Articles 598–604 CC).

Among the duties that the holder of the easement assumes, the carrying out of works necessary for the use and maintenance of the easement can be mentioned. These works must not alter the easement nor make it more onerous (Article 543 CC). If there are several dominant estates, the expenses should be proportional to the benefit that the easement gives to everyone. However, the one that does not want to contribute could renounce the easement in favour of the rest and therefore be exempted (Article 544 CC).

V. Extinction

160. Causes for extinction are provided in Article 546 CC. Among them is mentioned the consolidation (i.e., the effect that occurs when the owner of the servient estates becomes subsequently the owner of the dominant one, or vice versa),[100] the very unsatisfactory state of the estates at issue, the lack of use, and the holder's renouncement.

§7. Licenses

161. The free use or possession of immovable goods by mere tolerance of their owner is given the name of 'precarious' in Spanish Law. This term is also intended

96. *See* STS 30 Dec. 1975 (*RJA* 1975, 4846), STS 7 Jul. 1983 (*RJA* 1983, 4114), STS 13 May 1986 (*RJA* 1986, 2722), STS 7 Mar. 1991 (*RJA* 1991, 2079), STS 24 Feb. 1997 (*RJA* 1997, 1193).
97. *See* STS 22 Dec. 2008 (*RJA* 2009, 538).
98. *See* STS 14 Jul. 1995 (*RJA* 1995, 3708), STS 20 Jun. 2008 (*RJA* 2008, 3156).
99. *See* STS 16 May 1991 (*RJA* 1991, 3708), STS 20 Dec. 1997 (*RJA* 1997, 9337), STS 4 Jun. 2008 (*RJA* 2008, 3198).
100. *See* STS 28 Dec. 1964 (*RJA* 1964, 6298).

to describe the position of a person who remains in possession of a building, with acquiescence of the owner, after the extinction of the title that allowed him/her to use it (e.g., termination of the agreed period in a lease). Finally, the precarious result is similar to the position of the contracting partner who has signed a free loan when the obligation of returning the borrowed goods to the owner had not been subject to a definite deadline.

162. The precarious is not really a right. It does not mean a burden for the property, nor may it be opposed before future purchasers of the object so possessed. Moreover, it may not even be asserted against the current owner, as is shown by the fact that the Spanish Law on Civil Procedures (LEC) empowers the 'owner, holder of usufruct or any other person with right to possess the urban or rural property' to bring a judicial action against the 'holder' of the precarious to recover the possession of the immovable at issue (Article 250.2 LEC).

§8. Restrictive Covenants

163. The restrictive covenants (or 'negative easements') are defined in Article 533 CC as those in which the owner of the servient estate commits himself/herself to *non facere*, that is to say, not doing something that will be licit for him/her to do if the easement did not exist (e.g., not raising a construction or not raising it beyond a definite height). It is a burden with a negative content and indissolubly linked to the estate that it burdens. The holder may oppose the easement before anyone that becomes an owner of the servient estate, who will see how his/her ownership is limited because of the burden.

In Spanish Law, the distinction between positive and negative easements has significance above all with regard to usucapion, as the day when the usucapion term must start to run varies depending on the kind of easement. For positive easements, the *dies a quo* is the date on which the easement starts to be exercised, although for restrictive covenants the time starts to be calculated when the owner of the dominant estate forbids the owner of the servient estate the performance of the behaviour that would be licit in absence of easement, by means of a formal notification.

Chapter 5. Security Interests (*See Also Infra* Part V. Security).

164. The goal of 'guarantee real rights' (Spanish best denomination for 'security interests') is securing a credit through the granting to its holder (the creditor) of a power to demand the mandatory sale of a property (normally a debtor's property, but this may also be a third party's one), in order to be paid, before other creditors, with the money obtained in the auction (*see also* Parts II, IV and V).

The CC foresees basically two guarantee real rights: (1) the pledge that lies in movable goods and that gives the creditor the right to keep in his/her hands the goods that are the object of the right until the credit is completely satisfied (Articles 1863–1873 CC); and (2) the mortgage that lies in immovable goods and that does not give the creditor the right to keep possession of the goods that are the object of the right until the credit is completely satisfied (Articles 1874–1880 CC).[101]

165. Guarantee real rights have accessory nature in relation to the credit that they guarantee, which means that they cannot exist without a valid obligation that sustains them.

Although these rights give their holders the power to demand the mandatory sale of the goods in which they lie, they do not grant them the power to appropriate these goods directly. The alienation of the goods burdened with pledge or mortgage must be carried out through judicial or notarial procedures, provided legally.

166. The qualification of these rights as real rights has been questioned among scholars, mainly due to the lack of direct power over the object; for example, in the case of a mortgage, the holder of the right – mortgage creditor – has no possession of the mortgaged estate, which continues in its owner's hands (it may be either the debtor or a third party),[102] even though it must be observed that the power to demand the mandatory sale of the burdened object implies a possibility of action relevant enough as to appreciate the note of 'direct power' over the object, typical of real rights. Moreover, the pledge and the mortgage have doubtless the feature of *erga omnes* efficacy.

---

101. There are other rights of this nature foreseen in some special laws. It is the case of the movable mortgage right and the right of pledge without transfer of possession (*see* homonymous Law of 16 Dec. 1954). Both of them will be exhaustively analysed *infra* Parts II and V.

102. The person who mortgages an immovable belonging to his/her patrimony must not be, necessarily, the debtor of the guaranteed debt. On the other hand, the constitution of a mortgage does not eliminate the power of the mortgaged estate's owner to convey it freely. In the case of conveyance, the mortgage will continue to burden upon the estate, whoever the new owner is and provided that the right of mortgage is necessarily recorded in the Land Registry. For a more detailed study on this issue, *see infra* Part V, Ch. 1, §2.

Chapter 6. Joint Ownership

§1. Joint Ownership of Immovable Property

I. In General

167. Article 392 CC says that 'there is co-ownership when the ownership of an object or a right belongs *pro indiviso* to several people'. Statutory provisions for joint ownership are contained in Articles 392–406 CC, which apply not only to co-ownership in movable or immovable goods *stricto sensu* but also to joint ownership of any real right other from property.

The joint ownership described by these rules is the so-called Roman or by quotas joint ownership. It is characterized because every co-owner holds an aliquot part of the common object or right, which empowers him/her to obtain a portion of the object (or its price) at the moment of extinction and division of the joint ownership. Although the CC does not provide expressly for it, the co-ownership may have a legal or a contractual origin. The legal co-ownership is applicable when definite circumstances foreseen by a legal rule happen (e.g., the inheritors of a dead person have a joint ownership in the inheritance until the division of it). The contractual origin is created as a result of a contract agreed upon by two or more parties (e.g., purchase of a building by two or more buyers).

168. Every co-owner may freely use the common object, but in such a way that the other co-owners are neither affected in their interest in the object nor deprived of the same type of use (Article 394 CC).

In order to administrate and better enjoy the goods, majority agreements will be necessary, understanding that the CC does not speak of majority of people but of quotas, which means that the co-owner or co-owners who hold(s) the major part of the goods will be able to adopt the decisions on its management.[103] However, if such an agreement so adopted would be seriously damaging for the remaining co-owners, the interested parties might come before the judicial authority (Article 398 CC).[104]

169. Every co-owner has the right to oblige the others to contribute to the maintenance expenses of the common object and for it to be preserved in a state according to its agreed use (Article 395 CC). Every one of them must assume this obligation in proportion to his/her respective quota (Article 393 CC), although they are allowed to renounce his/her part of the object and therefore be exempted from the payment (Article 395 CC). This eventual renouncement will redound for the benefit of the other co-owners, always in proportion to their respective participation in the joint ownership.[105]

103. *See* STS 6 Mar. 1997 (*RJA* 1997, 1651).
104. *See* STS 25 February 2005 (*RJA* 2005, 4036).
105. F. Echeverría Summers, *Comentario a los Arts 392 a 406 CC, in Comentarios al Código Civil* 639 (R. Bercovitz Rodríguez-Cano, ed. Aranzadi 2013).

170. None of the co-owners, without consent of the others, may modify the common object, even in cases wherein the modification could bring about advantages for all of them (Article 397 CC).[106] The sale – or other types of alienation – of the common object/right also requires the unanimous consent of every co-holder, which may be express or tacit, previous or subsequent.[107]

Contrary to this, and provided that one is speaking of economic rights, every co-owner is able to transfer his/her individual quota or burden it freely (Article 399 CC).

171. Joint ownership can be extinguished because of several reasons (e.g., destruction of the goods), although the CC mentions only the extinction that occurs due to the division of the common object (*actio comuni dividundo*).

According to Article 400 CC, none of the co-owners is obliged to remain in the joint ownership, and every one of them may *at any time* request the division of the common object.[108] The CC contemplates, however, two exceptions to the exercise of the *actio comuni dividundo*, which are (a) the co-owners' agreement in order to maintain the joint ownership undivided; and (b) the objective indivisibility of the common object.

172. The validity of an indivisibility agreement is admitted by Article 400 CC, which requires that the indivision does not exceed the term of ten years, although an ulterior prorogation by means of a new agreement is allowed.

With regard to the second exception, Article 401 CC states that the co-owners may not demand the division of the common object when if divided 'it would be useless for the use to which it had been destined'. In accordance with the jurisprudence, the physical division of the common object is wrong not only when the object is indivisible by nature but also when it would be severely damaged (in an economic or legal sense) as a consequence of the division.[109]

173. When the common object is divisible, the parts resultant from the division have to be proportional to the quota of every co-owner. If it is an indivisible object, co-owners may agree its assignment to one of them, who would assume the obligation of compensating the rest proportionally. If an agreement cannot be reached, the object will be sold and the price divided among the co-owners (Article 404 CC).

174. There are three ways to carry out the division of the common goods:

(1) By contract: The co-owners themselves make the partition by common agreement (Article 402 CC).

106. *See* STS 8 May 2008 (*RJA* 2008, 2964).
107. *See* STS 14 Oct. 1998 (*RJA* 1998, 8374).
108. The jurisprudence (*v. gr.* STS 28 Mar. 2003 (*RJA* 2003, 3040)) shows that this action is imprescriptible.
109. *See* STS 11 May 1999 (*RJA* 1999, 4254), STS 3 Feb. 2005 (*RJA* 2005, 913).

(2) By arbitration: The co-owners ask a third party to make the division and to establish the part corresponding to every one (Article 402 CC). The third-party decision is mandatory for the co-owners.[110]

(3) By the judge: When there is no agreement to make the division by any of the previous procedures, the co-owners may ask the judicial authority to intervene.[111] According to Article 406 CC, the rules regarding the division of an inheritance (Articles 782–805 LEC) are applicable to this case.

175. The effects of the division are different for the co-owners and for the third parties:

(a) Co-owners acquire the autonomous and exclusive ownership of the part that has been given them after the division.

(b) The division cannot damage third parties, which means that they will keep the right (of mortgage, easement, and so on) in the goods (or in the different parts into which they have been divided) that belonged to them before the division was made (Article 405 CC).

II. Co-ownership Applied to Apartment Buildings

A. Joint Ownership of Blocks of Flats

176. The joint ownership of blocks of flats (which in Spanish Law is known as 'Horizontal Property') constitutes a special kind of property that comprises a mixed object: (a) on the one side, the so-called private or individual elements, that is to say, each and every one of the flats and premises of the block, liable to separate use and enjoyment, which have their own exit to a common element of the building or to the street; and (b) on the other side, a quota in the so-called common elements of the building (e.g., stairs, corridors, beams, walls, fronts, terraces, yards, conductions, drainages).[112]

The statutory provisions for this form of ownership can be found in Article 396 CC and, as an extension to it, in Law 49/1960 (21 July 1960), on Joint Ownership of Blocks of Flats (LPH), modified by Law 8/1999 (6 April 1999), LEC, Law 51/2003 (2 December 2003) and Law 8/2013 (8 June 2013). These provisions refer to the description of co-owners' rights and duties regarding individual and common elements, particularly the duty of contribution to general expenses relating to the maintenance of common elements. They also describe the procedures for adopting decisions in the bosom of the community of co-owners and the limits applicable to improvements made.

110. *See* STS 12 Jul. 1996 (*RJA* 1996, 5885).
111. *See* STS 30 Nov. 1988 (*RJA* 1988, 8727).
112. Article 396 CC defines these common elements as those necessary for the co-owners to use and enjoy the building in an adequate way.

The distinction between common and private elements has a great significance in relation to the use and alienation of each kind of element, as well as regarding maintenance and reparation costs.

177. The establishment of the joint ownership of a block of flats requires the granting of a juridical act known as 'constitutive title' (of the joint ownership of a block of flats). By means of this constitutive title, the sole owner of the building or the owners of the different flats and premises submit the building to this special kind of joint ownership. If registration in the Land Registry is desired, it must be stated in a notarial deed. According to Article 5 LPH, the constitutive title of this special property must contain both the description of the building as a whole and the description of each and every one of the flats and premises.[113]

Besides the constitutive title, it is also necessary to mention the bylaw, which is the set of rules given by the sole owner of the building, or by the owners of the different flats and premises unanimously. The bylaw is called to regulate use of the building or destiny, as well as other matters, such as expenses, administration and management, maintenance, insurances and reparations (Article 5 LPH). Nevertheless, granting it is purely voluntary, so if the bylaw is not approved, the legal suppletory provisions will simply be applied.

178. Article 3 LPH provides that a quota, referred to as the total value of the building, must be assigned to every one of the flats and premises in the constitutive title. The quota is expressed as a percentage. The criteria to fix this quota are the useful area of the flat or premises in proportion to the total area of the building, its inside or outside location, the floor, and the use of the services or common elements that can be rationally supposed to be made by the owner of the flat at issue (Article 5 LPH).

The quota also functions as a parameter to fix the ratio in which every owner must assume burdens and benefits linked to its position within the joint ownership. Unless a different system is agreed upon,[114] all of the co-owners are obliged to contribute according to their quota to the expenses made for the adequate maintenance of the building and its services, burdens and responsibilities.

The quotas must be recorded in the constitutive title, which means that they may be fixed or modified only by the sole owner of the building or by all of the owners unanimously, always according to the statutory criteria.

179. In his/her flat or premises, every owner may carry out works that he/she considers necessary, provided that these works neither damage the safety of the building, its structure or its outward appearance, nor harm the rights of other owners (Article 7 LPH). It is necessary the approval of three-fifths of the Owners Assembly, apart from an administrative authorization, to make the division of a flat or premises, as well as the subsequent fixation of new quotas (Article 10.3.b/LPH).

113. *See* STS 3 Feb. 1975 (*RJA* 1975, 326) and STS 13 Apr. 1977 (*RJA* 1977, 1652).

114. *See* Art. 9.1.e) LPH. The STS 10 Mar. 1993 (*RJA* 1993, 1788) gave validity to an agreement by means of which the co-owners had decided to support equally the costs of maintenance of the building.

Private elements are liable to alienation, which must be done together with the participation corresponding to every flat or premises in relation to the common elements of the building (Article 3 LPH, *in fine*).

In respect to the owner's duties, one must note the duty to refrain from carrying out activities in the flat or premises that (a) may be harmful to the building; (b) are forbidden according to the bylaw; or (c) go against general rules on annoying, unhealthy, harmful, dangerous or illicit activities (Article 7 LPH). Moreover, the owners do have the duty to preserve their flats or premises in a good state, as well as other private elements (e.g., junk rooms, garages), in order to avoid injuries to the remaining owners or to common elements. They must even consent that their private elements are subject to reparations imposed by building service (Article 9.1.b) and c) LPH).

The owners have the right to use the common elements, such as the power to alienate their quota in them, together with the alienation of their flat or premises. They may not modify any common element, and they are obliged to contribute to the building maintenance expenses, including its services, burdens and responsibilities, provided that all of them are not liable to individualization (Article 9 LPH).

180. The joint ownership of a block of flats comprises several governing bodies of administration, management and government, which are the Chairman, the Vice-chairman, the Administrator, the Secretary and the Owners' Assembly.

The Chairman holds the representation of the joint ownership's members, in and outside court, with regard to all kind of issues that may affect them (Article 13.2 LPH). The Vice-chairman substitutes for the Chairman in the case of his/her absence, vacancy or inability to serve.

The charge of Administrator may be occupied by the Chairman, unless the bylaw, or the Owners' Assembly by majority agreement, provides the need for a different appointment. Among the Administrator's competences are the development of a budget and the care of building maintenance, including the power to order the carrying out of urgent repairs.

The Secretary is responsible for drawing up the records of the Owners' Assembly, as well as taking care of all books and documents of the joint ownership. The Chairman may function as Secretary, if no other person is appointed to this role.

The Owners' Assembly is the body that joins together all the owners who have flats or premises in the building. The Assembly is responsible for the appointment and removal of all the other members of the governing body. It is also in charge of approving the bylaw and the budgets, as well as resolving any issue of interest on behalf of the owners as a whole.

181. Apart from the destruction of the building, the conversion of the joint ownership of the block into a model of ordinary ownership or co-ownership is contemplated in Article 23 LPH as causes of extinction of the joint ownership of a block of flats.

B. Private Building Complexes

182. Besides the joint ownership of a block of flats, the LPH (Article 24) mentions the so-called private building complexes, which can be defined as a collection of buildings, each one eventually constituted by flats and premises. These complexes include, together with the common elements of each building, other common elements or services for the benefit of the whole collection of buildings that compose every complex.[115]

183. There are two types of organization for private building complexes. The first one is the constitution of a single general joint ownership, composed of all the owners of flats and premises corresponding to all the different buildings included in the complex, which would be submitted to the statutory provisions in the LPH. The second possibility is the creation of a group of joint ownerships in such a manner that every building would maintain its own management and government bodies.

With regard to the common elements of the complex (e.g., roads, gardens and sport areas), a General Assembly could be created, whose members would be the Chairmen of the joint ownerships corresponding to every building in the complex. The General Assembly and the assemblies of every building will have their own competences: The former would limit itself to the management of the elements and services that are common to the whole complex, without interfering with the field of the latter.

C. The Right of Exploitation in Shifts of Buildings for Use by Tourism

184. In Spain, time-sharing is known as 'exploitation in shifts of buildings for use by tourism'. At first, the corresponding right was regulated in Law 42/1998 (15 December 1998), in which Directive 94/47/CE (26 October 1994) was incorporated into Spanish Law. But now the Law in force is Law 4/2012 (6 July) (LCAT), which is a transposition of Directive 2008/112/CE (14 January). This latter Directive, which has derogated the former Directive of 1994, is aimed at achieving a higher harmonization in this field. New contractual formulas have been regulated in order to increase the consumer's protection. The same goal is seemed to be sought through the reinforcement of the pre-contractual information obligations. The regulation of the consumer's withdrawal within the period of fourteen days after the contract's signature has been considerably amplified, as well as the prohibition for the entrepreneur (transferor of one of these rights) to ask him any kind of payment before this period. The current Spanish Law is divided into three Sections (Titles I, II and III). The first one is devoted in part to the regulation of these new juridical formulas that are covered by the European Directive of 2008. The third one comprises taxation rules. And Title II contains the regulation of the exploitation in shifts

115. J.L. Lacruz Berdejo et al., *Elementos de Derecho Civil III. Derechos Reales*, vol. 2 459 et seq (Dykinson 2009).

of buildings by use of tourism. This right gives its holder the power to enjoy, exclusively for a specific period every year, a tourist accommodation together with adequate furniture for the use of it (Article 23.1).

Before the publication of the prior Law of 1998, Spanish scholars normally designed this phenomenon as 'multi-ownership', configuring this right as a form of undivided co-ownership in an estate. Currently, however, the Law states that the right of exploitation in shifts of buildings for use by tourism cannot be mistaken for the ownership of the estate that it burdens. In this sense, Article 23.4 LCAT provides that 'the real right of exploitation in shifts can be in no way assimilated to an undivided quota of ownership, or called "multi-ownership" or in any other way that contains the term *ownership*'. The right of exploitation in shifts of buildings for use by tourism consists of an actual limited real right in another one's goods (*iura in re aliena*) but can be shaped as a personal lease too (Article 23.6 LCAT). It is even possible to include within this category (and therefore within the Law of 2012) another contract aimed at providing accommodation to the transferee for more than one period of time, provided that the contract lasts at least for one year. This right may be registered in the Land Registry according to Articles 2 LH and 7 RH.

185. The right of exploitation in shifts of buildings for use by tourism may fall upon a building, a building complex, or an area architecturally differentiated within them, provided that it is composed of a minimum of ten different independent accommodations (Article 23.2 LCAT). The legitimation to constitute this right corresponds to the owner or owners of the building, complex or area, by means of the granting of a notarial deed and the subsequent registration in the Land Registry (Article 25 LCAT).

186. The right of exploitation in shifts of buildings for use by tourism is purchased through a contract that, for the protection of the purchaser, must be put in writing (Article 30.1 LCAT). The compensation payable to the transferor comprehends both the price for the acquisition of the right and an annual amount allotted to the service company that takes care of the building's cleaning and maintenance (or to the owner, if he/she takes care of these activities).

Until the fourteenth day after the signature of the contract as a general rule, the purchaser may freely rescind it (only in the case that he/she can be considered as a consumer – relations business-to-business are excluded of this free withdraw –), without being obliged to pay any compensation or expenses at all (Articles 12.1 and 31.2 LCAT). He/she has also the power to extinguish the contract, should it not fulfil the minimum content and form requirements mentioned in Article 30 LCAT.

The owner, on his/her side, also has the right to extinguish the contract when the acquirer does not pay the quotas for services corresponding to one year.

187. The right of exploitation in shifts of buildings for use by tourism empowers its holder to use the accommodation for a period of time that cannot be shorter than seven consecutive days each year. The shifts must not have equal duration. But, in any case, a free period of seven days must be kept between every shift in order to carry out accommodation maintenance and cleaning works (Article 23.3 LCAT). As said, these activities must be done by a service company or by the owner himself/herself.

The holder may use his/her right with no more limits than the legal ones, and the alienation of the right does not affect the duties coming from statutory provisions (Article 33.1 LCAT).

§2. JOINT OWNERSHIP OF MOVABLE PROPERTY

188. The provisions on co-ownership contained in Articles 392–406 CC also apply when two or more people appear as co-owners or co-holders of a real limited right on movable goods, for which in this section one simply refers to what has been said above (*see supra* §1).

Chapter 7. Neighbourhood and Urban Problems

189. The term *neighbourly relations* relates to the content of a set of rules that limits the property and other real rights. These rules are aimed at achieving the peaceful coexistence among owners of close or nearby estates. The notion of 'neighbourhood' and accordingly the notion of 'neighbourly relations' are exclusively applicable to the field of estates because the neighbourhood refers to a permanent tie of contiguity between two things, impossible to find in the field of movables, which are by definition liable to movement.

The concern about guaranteeing good relations between neighbours already appeared in Roman Law, when the thesis that the owner of an estate may not disturb holders of nearby estates by allowing strange elements, fluids or gases into their estates started to be admitted (*immissio*).

In the Middle Ages the concern continued, although the rules regulating the neighbourly relations were led by the 'emulation theory', according to which only the damaging acts that, without providing any value to the owner, were done with the exclusive goal of causing harm to the neighbour were worthy of forbiddance.

With the advent of the Industrial Revolution, this theory appeared clearly insufficient to avoid the increase of risk and damages stemming from technological progress. Thus, new theories were formulated, as the 'normal tolerance' one created by the famous German scholar Rudolph von Ihering. This author defended the prohibition of any interference, either direct or indirect, in the neighbouring estate that exceeded normal tolerance, although made with no intention of damaging.

190. The influence of Ihering's theory in Spanish Law may be appreciated in Articles 590 and 1908.2 CC. Article 590 CC provides that 'nobody may construct near someone else's wall, or near a dividing one, wells, drains, aqueducts, kilns, forges, chimneys, cowsheds, deposits of corrosive materials, artifacts moved by vapour or fabrics that by themselves or by their products are dangerous or noxious, without maintaining the mandatory distances fixed in regulations and uses of the area, and without conducting the necessary safeguards, subject to the conditions prescribed by regulations. If a regulation has not been prescribed, the precautions considered necessary will be taken, after an expert's opinion, to avoid any damage to the neighbouring estate or building'. Article 1908.2 CC provides that the owners will be responsible for damages caused by 'excessive visible vapours, which are noxious to persons or properties'.

191. There are also some other rules given in order to avoid the conflicts derived from the close coexistence of estates.

Thus, within the regulation of legal easements in the CC, there are several articles whose content has nothing to do with the constitution of burdens upon a property but are purely legal limits to property imposed because of a neighbourhood between estates. Contrary to easements, established on an estate for the benefit of another, and in need of an expressed act of establishment, the limits to property come directly from the law, which provides them with the aim of directing the coexistence between neighbouring owners better. Moreover, limits have a reciprocal character, in the sense that the behaviours or abstentions that they impose may be requested reciprocally between the affected owners.[116]

Other limitations are regulated in the laws on joint ownership of blocks of flats and on urban leases. Article 7.2 LPH foresees that neither the owner, nor the occupant of the flat or premises, may 'develop in it or in any other part of the building activities forbidden by the bylaw, which are damaging to the property or contrary to general rules on annoying, unhealthy, harmful, dangerous or illicit activities'. Article 27.1.e) LAU provides for, as resolution cause for the lease at the lessor's request, the development of 'annoying, unhealthy, harmful, dangerous or illicit activities' in the house.

116. Some of the limits set in the CC because of neighbourly relations, affect the minimum distance that must be observed when planting trees (Art. 591 CC) or opening windows and balconies (Arts 580–584 CC). Other ones refer to the measures that may be taken when a neighbouring tree or building is about to fall down (Arts 389–390 CC). There are also limits that foresee the duty for every owner to build his/her building's roof in such a way that rainwater falls upon his/her own property, or upon the street or other public place, but not upon the neighbour's estate (Art. 586 CC).

Chapter 8. Agrarian Problems

192. See supra Part I, Chapter 2. Legal Interests, § 2. Immovable Property, IV. Agrarian Property.

Part II. Movable Property and Personal Property: Chattels

Chapter 1. General Classification

193. The Spanish CC does not consider a distinction between 'Real Property' and 'Personal Property',[117] but categories of movable property and immovable property can be found.[118] Within the former, it is still possible to distinguish depending on whether the object of the right has a tangible or an intangible nature.

Traditionally, movable goods have been characterized, from a legal point of view, depending on their aptitude for being moved from one place to another. In this sense, Article 335 CC indicates that 'they are considered movable goods (…) in general all those that are liable to be moved from one point to another without damage to the immovable thing to which they were joined'. The CC includes here an open clause instead of a detailed catalogue, although due to other provisions, it is possible to conclude the movable nature of money, jewellery, securities, claims, books, weapons, medals, scientific or artistic collections, clothes, cars, grain, liquid-good stuffs, as well as furniture (Article 346 CC).

Despite the fact that they are, in general, corporeal things, liable to possessory taking, incorporeal objects, as claims, specifically rents and pensions (Article 336 CC), are also included, without forgetting *iura in re aliena* concerning movable goods (Article 334.10 CC connected to Article 335 CC).

§1. Tangible Movable Property and Choses in Possession

194. Tangible movable goods are those characterized by their corporeity, that is to say, perceptible objects, defined in the space and physically seizable by means of possession. The feature indicated in Article 335 CC (liability to moving) is fully applicable to this kind of movables.

117. *See supra* Part I, Ch. 1.
118. The significance of the object of the right of property (or any other real right) being movable or immovable has already been pointed out. Subjects such as publicity of the right or requirements for alienation differ depending on goods having a movable or an immovable nature. Generally, immovables receive a more severe treatment by the law, which is justified because in the codification age, they were the assets endowed with more economic value.

195. As regards tangible movable goods, there are two classical classifications: The first one distinguishes between consumable and non-consumable goods, and the second one between fungible and non-fungible goods. Article 337 CC defines fungible goods as 'those ones whose normal use causes its consumption', which is pretty equivocal because that definition refers better to the concept of consumable goods. On the contrary, non-consumable goods are those that simply wear out as a result of its normal use.

From other provisions in the CC (e.g., Article 1448 or Article 1452), one can infer that the attribute of 'fungible' consists of the identity that all the objects belonging to a same group have – due to this, the possibility of exchange or substitution among them within trade follows. A classic example is money.

Non-fungible goods, on the contrary, would be those not replaceable by others with equivalent features belonging to the same class. They may also be called 'definite goods' or 'specific goods'. Mostly, there are not *absolutely* but *relatively* fungible or non-fungible goods because it is always possible to imagine a hypothetical class that an object could belong to, although *a priori* it seemed unique.

§2. Intangible Movable Property and Choses in Action

196. Immaterial goods form a singular category of movable goods and, as such, are the object of regulation by means of special laws, as the Law on Intellectual Property (12 April 1996), the Law on Patents (24 July 2015 (LP)) and the Law on Trademarks (7 December 2001 (LM)). They are denominated 'immaterial (or "intangible" or "incorporeal") goods' because they are mere intellectual entities, which receive the name of 'goods' by virtue of a legal fiction. Within this category, intellectual creations *lato sensu*, with or without industrial nature, are included. It is clear that the legal protection for intellectual creations is autonomous from that one corresponding to the material objects in that the former are, eventually, fixed.

In Spain, unlike Common Law countries, the expression *intellectual property* is reserved to objects – works – protected by copyright, as well as to related objects (performances and productions of works). The expression *industrial property* is applicable both to objects protected by a patent or similar right (e.g., inventions, designs) and to objects protected as trademarks and trade names.

197. Authors acquire intellectual property by means of the creation of his/her work. The sole requisite for protection is the work's originality. Any additional condition, as official deposit or registration is not required. A work is original if not copied from another and raised enough over the public domain elements. It is indistinct if the work is not materialized in a tangible support. The author is legally vested in a suit of rights upon his/her work. On the one hand, there are 'moral' rights (e.g., right to decide the moment and way of the work's publication), and on the other hand, there are rights with an 'economic' (or 'patrimonial') content (e.g., right to authorize the reproduction and distribution of the work). Although the former are inalienable and non-renounceable rights, the latter may be (and frequently are) transferred to third parties by virtue of contracts.

Intellectual property is subjected to a legal deadline (seventy years), which starts from the author's death or from the work's publication (depending on several circumstances). Even during the period of legal protection, intellectual property rights are subjected to severe limitations in order to favour some social interests and political liberties. Although there is an Intellectual Property Registry in Spain, recording the works has a mere declarative value, the acquisition of the right not being subjected to the previous registration. Spain has signed the Berne Convention (for the Protection of Literary and Artistic Works), and has also signed the World Intellectual Property Organization Treaties on Copyright and on Performances and Phonograms (1996).

198. Patents constitute the first category within industrial property rights. According to Article 4 LP, 'in all fields of technology new inventions may be patented that involve an inventive activity and are liable to an industrial application'. The granting of a patent right is the competence of the Industrial Property Registry, where the granting must be applied for. The right has a duration (that cannot be prorogued) of twenty years, starting from the date of the request. Although the right belongs to the inventor or his/her inheritors, its alienation to third parties is possible by means of exploitation licenses. A patent right, for a shorter legal protection term, is also recognized in favour of people whose inventive activity consists of giving a new shape or structure to a pre-existing object resulting in an appreciable profit for its use or fabrication (Article 137 LP).

The category of designs that in Spanish Law are known as 'industrial designs' should also be mentioned. This category includes the external appearance of the whole or a part of a product coming from the characters of, in particular, its lines, outlines, colours, shape, texture, materials of the product by itself or of its ornamentation (Article 1.2(a) Law on Juridical Protection of Industrial Design (Law 20/2003, 7 July) (LPJDI)). The granting of the right upon industrial designs must also be requested before the Designs Registry. Its legal protection ends after a five-year term, renewable for subsequent similar terms, until a maximum period of twenty-five years (Article 43 LPJDI).

Finally, there are trademarks, trade names and commercial establishments' labels whose regulation is located in the LM. The most important right among them is the one corresponding to trademarks. Although this right originated through its recording in the Industrial Property Registry, the user of a renowned non-registered trademark is qualified by the law to demand the nullity of a registered trademark liable to create confusion with his/her own trademark, provided that the action is exercised within a five-year term after the publication date of the registered trademark.

In Spanish Law, the trademark is not essentially linked to the company it belongs to, which means that the trademark may be alienated separately from the latter. The holder of a trademark right is obliged to use the trademark, directly or through a third party, because – for want of use, without just cause, and for an uninterrupted term of five years – the law foresees the expiration of the right and the cancellation of its record.

§3. FUNDS

199. Within this section, securities, distinguishing between securities representing a credit and securities representing the sharing of someone in a company's capital (shares), will be considered.

200. With securities, something very similar occurs as it does to money: the conversion of an immaterial good, such as a right of credit, into a material good, which is incorporated into a tangible document. Securities, representing a credit, incorporate a promise to carry out a defined contribution (i.e., the payment of an amount of money or the delivery of goods) in favour of the person who appears as the legitimate holder of the document. This incorporation produces the materialization of the credit in such a manner that from that moment, the credit may circulate within the traffic as the rest of movable goods, without need of fulfilment of the basic rules for the transfer of personal rights (Articles 1526 et seq. CC).

Securities may be the object of different kinds of contracts (i.e., sale, donation, and exchange) and it is also possible to constitute upon them limited real rights (i.e., usufruct and pledge). However, the traffic of securities depends on the type they belong to: 'nominal', 'bearer' or 'to the order'. First, nominal securities designate in the document itself the person specifically legitimate to request the amount to which the credit extends. The traffic of these securities requires the notification of the transmission to the debtor, together with the delivery of the document to the acquirer.

Second, bearer securities do not contain the designation of the credit's owner, being legitimate to exercise the right against the debtor the person who holds the document at a definite time. Its transfer follows the general rules given for movable goods, which means that both an alienation contract and the delivery of the document to the acquirer are needed.[119] It is therefore not necessary, contrary to the previous case, to notify the credit's conveyance to the debtor.

Finally, securities to the order are those in which the credit may be requested to the order of the document's first drawee or to the order of the person who appears designated in the document as the last acquirer or legitimate holder. A typical example is the bill of exchange, which incorporates a payment order made by the drawer in favour of the drawee in the same document. The bill of exchange is liable to be transferred through a conveyance called 'endorsement', which is reflected by a signal in the bill of exchange as a declaration of the drawer that orders to pay the credit (incorporated into the bill of exchange) to the person designed in the document (endorsee), who may endorse the bill to a third party and so on. This also means that the securities to the order circulate according to the general rules of acquisition of real rights, without the need to notify the credit's transfer to the debtor/drawer.

201. Besides the securities, the titles representing the sharing of someone in a company's capital must also be mentioned. The 'shares' are participation units within a limited-liability company's capital, and they are granted to someone, in a

---

119. On this issue, *see infra* Part III.

greater or smaller number, in exchange for his/her contribution to the company. The share gives its owner the 'shareholder' condition, which implies a set of rights regulated by law (Ccom) and Law on Companies (LSC). Among these rights, the right to participate in the sharing out of benefits and the patrimony after liquidation, the right to assist and vote in the General Meeting of shareholders, or the subscription on a pre-emptive basis right of new shares issued by the company should be mentioned.

The LSC foresees that the shares may be materialized in documents (securities *stricto sensu*) or through book-entry securities (Article 921 LSC).

The traditional system is the representation of the share through a document that incorporates the shareholder's rights. These rights can be transmitted to third parties by means of the delivery of the document and the fulfilment of some specific legal duties depending on the type of share. Shares materialized in documents may be 'nominal' or 'bearer' (Article 113 LSC). The first ones designate their owner in the document itself, although the bearer shares legitimate for the exercise of the rights to the person who holds the document at a definite time. Both types of shares are liable to be conveyed according to the rules stated for movable goods, that is, by means of an alienation contract followed by the delivery of the document into the acquirer's hands.

In the case of bearer securities, the validity of the transfer also requires the intervention of a notary or a mediation society specifically accredited to act within the Securities Market. When the shares are nominal, the transfer must be communicated to the company for it to register the conveyance.

The book-entry security is a method of representation that was introduced in Spain by the Law on the Securities Market (TRLMV) (28 July 1988, LMV), and is currently foreseen in Article 91.2 LSC and Article 6 TRLMV (recast text of the Law on Securities Market 23 October 2015). The book-entry security avoids the incorporation of the share into a document, which is substituted by a record made in an accounting electronic register. However, Article 92.1 LSC states that these book-entry securities also have the condition of 'movable securities'. Nevertheless, the transfer of this kind of shares does not follow the classical scheme of acquisition for movable goods foreseen in Spanish legal order, according to which both a title (i.e., contract) and the delivery of the object to the transferee are necessary (*see* Article 609 CC). In these cases, the system is hugely simplified because the shareholder condition can be transferred by means of a simple accounting entry. The book-entry security can be the object of limited real rights, which is coherent with its designation as movable security (Article 12 TRLMV).

§4. Chattels Personal and Chattels Real

202. This subject is not applicable in Spanish Law.

Chapter 2. Legal Interests

203. As occurs in the field of real estate,[120] Spanish Law does not follow in the matter of movable goods the distinction between 'legal' and 'equitable' interests. By influence of Roman Law, the Spanish CC adheres to the classification that distinguishes between the right of property and the limited real rights, or rights in another person's goods (*iura in re aliena*).

§1. Movable Property

204. Article 348 CC defines *property* as the right to enjoy and dispose of an object (movable or immovable) without more limitations than those established by the laws. However, the CE (Article 33) states the right to private property without making any distinction depending on the movable or immovable nature of the right's object. Article 33 CE adds to that statement by pointing out the private property's social function, which makes private property useful not only to the owner but also to the community. Because of this social function, every owner has to bear a series of limitations that determines the exercise of his/her right.[121]

Before the passing of the CE, the private property's social function was stated, always in the field of real estate, by the TRLS of 1956 and the LRDA of 1973. Both laws imposed a series of duties and limitations linked to their right of property to the owners of estates, either urban or rural, justified because of a social function. Thus began the acceptance of the existence of a special legal regulation applicable to immovable property, a regulation that was hugely different from the one reflected in Article 348 CC. On the contrary, movable goods continued to be fully subjected to the CC, therefore their owners kept no such limited powers over them.

This situation changed with the enactment of the CE in 1978 because it extended the private property's social function to any kind of goods. Because of this, it may be said also that movable property comprises two different faces, an individual and a social one. Hence, in view of the social function, some statutory restrictions on their right can be imposed on the owners of movable goods. However, STC 37/1987 (26 March 1987) stated that not all goods are able to give the same kind of utilities to the community, but the role of real estate, as the physical basis for several significant economic sectors (agriculture, industry, construction), is greater than the one corresponding to movable goods. This circumstance justifies the larger number of laws regulating land, both urban and agrarian.

205. However, movable property is, as it occurs with the immovable one, liable to be defended by means of the *vindicatio*, action that may be brought by the person who alleges to be the object's owner against the person in possession, who (in the plaintiff's opinion) holds the object without title. However, contrary to the immovable's *vindicatio*, the owner must prove here not only his/her acquisition act but also

120. *See supra* Part I, para. 86.

121. On property's social function, in the light of Art. 33 CE, *see supra* General Introduction, III.A, para. 41, as well as *supra* Part I, Ch. 1, §2, I, para. 91.

that the thing still continues to belong to him/her. Therefore, the presumption that the object's ownership is maintained by the person who acquired it at a definite past time does not apply in this context. Nevertheless, it can be enough that the owner proves that he/she lost the object or that somebody appropriated/stole it for the defendant – current possessor – to be obliged to return it.

§2. Movable Limited Real Rights

206. Limited real rights may fall upon both immovable and movable goods. The applicable regulation is basically the same,[122] although some nuances must be taken into account:

(a) There are some limited real rights that may have only as their objects immovable goods. This is in the case of building and planting rights, habitation/occupation, emphyteusis and rent charges, as well as easements. On the contrary, other real rights have an exclusively movable nature, as, for example, the pledge.[123] Finally, there are limited real rights that may have as their objects both movable and immovable goods (e.g., usufruct, use, and leases).
(b) Within the group of real rights, indistinctly applicable both to movable and immovable goods, the statutory provisions differ depending on the right falling upon one or other kinds of things. It is thus, for example, in the case of leases. The ones whose objects are immovable goods are subjected to the special statutory provisions contained either in the LAU or in the LAR.[124] On the contrary, the movable leases are merely subjected to the CC provisions (Articles 1542 et seq. CC). Another case would be the one of the guarantee rights, which are also subjected to different legal rules depending on the (movable or immovable) nature of the goods upon which they fall.

I. Guarantee Real Rights in Movables

207. Among the guarantee real rights on movables, the pledge, the movable mortgage, the pledge without transfer of possession, and the retention right could be mentioned (*see also* Part V). In comparison to immovable guarantee rights, they show significant nuances related to their content, constitution form and publicity. These nuances will be studied in detail *infra* Part V, Chapter 2.

122. *See supra* Part I, Ch. 4.
123. *See infra* Part V, Ch. 2.
124. *See supra* Part I, Ch. 4, §3.

II. Movable Leases

A. *In General*

208. The lease grants its holder the right to use temporarily another person's goods in exchange for a definite price (*see also* Part I). The legal provisions for the lease on movable goods are contained in Articles 1542 et seq. CC. Unlike the special laws on immovable urban and rural leases, the CC states the principle of freedom in fixing the length of the right, and it imposes no mandatory prorogation for the benefit of the lessee.

209. The content of the lessee's right can be summarized in the following chart of rights and duties:

(a) The lessee must use the goods diligently, according to the purpose for which they have been leased (Article 1555.2 CC).
(b) The lessee is obliged to preserve the leased object and to give it back at the end of the contract in the same state the object was when the lease started (Article 1561 CC).[125] The lessee suffers the burden of proving that the object was already impaired when received by him/her because the CC assumes that the object has been delivered to him/her in a good state (Article 1562 CC).[126]
(c) Repairs necessary to maintain the object must be paid by the lessor. However, it is the lessee – as possessor of the object – who must communicate to the lessor, within the shortest possible deadline, the need of carrying out these repairs. Otherwise, he/she will be liable for the damages caused to the owner as a result of his/her negligence (Article 1559 CC).
(d) The lessee is obliged to pay the lessor a price ('rent') in exchange for the temporary use of the leased object.
(e) Article 1573 CC implicitly allows the lessee to carry out works to improve the leased object. These improvements may be withdrawn by the lessee at the end of the contract, provided that with this action no damage will be caused to the leased object.

B. *'Leasing'*

210. In Spanish Law, the word *leasing* is applied to a contract not completely typified, subjected to a fragmentary legal treatment. In the field of movable goods, an additional provision contained in the Law on Discipline and Intervention of Credit Organizations (19 July 1988), as well as the Law on Sale on Credit of Movable Goods (13 July 1998 (LVPBM)), is applicable.

By means of this 'leasing' contract, a company (called the 'leasing company') obliges itself to give another undertaking the use of goods (normally, industrial

125. *See* STS 21 Jul. 1997 (*RJA* 1997, 5518).
126. On this subject, *see* STS 6 May 1994 (*RJA* 1994, 3715), STS 8 Nov. 1999 (*RJA* 1999, 8808), and STS 12 Feb. 2001 (*RJA* 2001, 850).

vehicles and machinery) for a definite period of time, in exchange for a periodical fee. At the end of the agreed-upon period, the user must choose among the following options: (a) to renew the contract setting the payment of a smaller fee; (b) to give the goods back to the leasing company; (c) to acquire the goods by a remaining price fixed in advance.

Mostly, the signature of this kind of contract is preceded by a proposal that the user makes to the leasing company for the latter to buy a definite thing and afterwards to transfer its use to the former in exchange for the payment of a rent. The legal nature of the 'leasing' is a topic under discussion within Spanish scholars. Two theories have been defended: (1) the 'leasing' involves an authentic sale on credit; and (2) the 'leasing' is not much more than a lease with an option of purchase accessory clause.

'Leasing' contracts may be the object of registration in the Registry of Movable Goods, although neither the efficacy of the contractual relationship nor the acquisition of the right to use the object depends on this fact.

Chapter 3. Equitable Interests

211. This subject is not applicable in Spanish Law.

Chapter 4. Security Interests

212. See infra Part V. Security. Chapter 2. Securities in Movable Property.

Chapter 5. The Publicity of Movable Real Rights

§1. The Role of Possession

213. Possession has always fulfilled a significant role in order to get the legal publicity of property and limited real rights on movable goods because it is a way to show before third parties the existence of these rights. Although in the field of immovable goods possession carries out a secondary function, being that the legal publicity is mainly implemented through the recording of the rights in the Land Registry, in the sphere of movables, because of their fewer probabilities of identification and individualization, their publicity rests mainly on the possession.

This point of view is reflected in Articles 448 and 464 CC. According to the first of them, 'the possessor is legally presumed to possess the goods on the basis of a just title, and nobody is allowed to force him/her to show it'. Therefore, the possession itself legitimates the possessor of movable goods in such a manner that everyone who claims the goods will be obliged to prove that the defendant is not actually legitimated to keep the goods under his/her power.

Article 464 CC intends to protect the third party, transferee of movable goods, who, being in good faith, has trusted in the actual ownership of his/her transferor, because he/she was the person who was in possession of the goods at the time the alienation took place. The protection coming from this legal provision results in guaranteeing that, given the mentioned conditions, the hypothetical *vindicatio* brought by the actual owner against the transferee will not succeed.[127]

§2. The Registry of Movable Goods

214. The Law on Movable Mortgage and Pledge without Transfer of Possession (16 December 1954 (LHMPDP)) introduced two new figures of real guarantees upon movable goods that continue to be currently in force (*see also* Part V).

Like the traditional pledge (*pignus*), these guarantees give its respective holder (creditor) a preference for collection related to the value of the burdened movable, in case the debtor does not fulfil his/her duty of payment. However, unlike the (ordinary) pledge, they do not require the creditor's possession of the goods. With this system, the lawmaker intended to give a solution to the problem, typical of the (ordinary) pledge, consisting in taking away from the debtor's hands the possession of the burdened goods, which in many cases was the only source of the debtor's revenues (i.e., the vehicle of a carrier).

Both movable mortgage and pledge without transfer of possession may fall only upon the categories of movable goods mentioned in the Law. These movable goods are characterized by being almost identifiable and individualized as immovable

127. Here one has a case of acquisition *a non domino* (*see infra* Part III, Ch. 3, §2), very similar to the one that may happen in the field of immovable goods in accordance with Art. 34 LH (*see supra* Part I, Ch. 2, §1). However, in the case of immovable goods, the protected appearance arises from the Land Registry's publicity.

goods.[128] Because of this circumstance, and the absence of publicity based on the possessory delivery in creditor's hands, the LHMPDP itself created a special Registry of Movable Mortgage and Pledge without Transfer of Possession. Unlike Land Registry, its goal was not the publication of the rights (property or other limited real rights) upon the registered goods but the publication of the contracts whose object was the constitution of a movable mortgage or a pledge without transfer of possession, as well as the seizure of goods liable to those two guarantees. Currently, the Registry of Movable Mortgage and Pledge without Transfer of Possession has been merged into the modern Registry of Movable Goods.

215. Years after the enactment of the LHMPDP, the possibility of registration for movable goods was extended to the contracts of sale on credit of movable goods, first regulated by the LVPBM of 17 July 1965, currently replaced by the homonymous law of 13 July 1998. The aim of this Law is endowing these kinds of contracts with a special status, wherein one of the contracting parties gives the other a corporeal movable non-consumable and identifiable object in exchange for a definite price that will be totally or partially paid on credit for a period not longer than three months starting from the signing of the contract. By way of guarantee, the LVPBM forbids the purchaser to transfer the object before he/she has paid the total price.

The contracting parties may also agree on a retention of title-clause, whereby the transfer of the possession of the goods will be delayed in such a manner that the seller will continue to be the owner until the buyer pays the total price. The opposability before third parties of these two guarantee mechanisms requires that the contract be registered in the Registry of Sale on Credit of Movable Goods, established by the LVPBM.

In its original form, the Registry of Sale on Credit of Movable Goods was a mere registry of burdens for sale on credit contracts guaranteed by means of either a forbiddance to transfer or a retention of title-clause. In the LVPBM of 1998, however, the scope of this Registry was extended in order to allow the registration of judiciary actions on ownership whose objects were movable goods sold on credit.

As in the case of movable mortgage and pledge without transfer of possession, the Registry of Sale on Credit of Movable Goods has been merged into the newer Registry of Movable Goods that has been established by the regulation on standard-form contracts, contained in the Royal Decree 1828/1999 (3 December 1999). Despite everything, the statutory provisions on Land Registry are applicable in a suppletory way.[129]

216. Unlike its immediate precedents, the Registry of Movable Goods gives publicity to every kind of title (not only burdens). Therefore, every act or contract

128. Liable to movable mortgage, for example, are motor vehicles, airships, and industrial machinery. As regards the pledge without transfer of possession, it falls upon objects whose place of location is mentioned in the constitutive title of the right in such a way that it is prohibited for the debtor to move them from that place without creditor's permission (Art. 60 LHMPDP).

129. For example, the principles of non-opposability before third parties for non-registered rights (Art. 32 LH) and protection for the appearance stemming from Registry entries (Art. 34 LH), both of them studied *supra* Part I, Ch. 2, § 1, are also applicable in this field.

related to identifiable movable goods, such as sales (with or without delayed price), ordinary or special leases, movable mortgages, pledges without transfer of possession, naval mortgages, claims, or seizures may be recorded.

As regards its structure, the Registry of Movable Goods is very close to the Land Registry. Its organization lies in the same system according to which a 'leaf' is assigned per item. Every 'leaf' in the Registry book contains the complete record of a definite item, in such a way that the examination of the Registry's books gives enough information about the good's current owner, the people to whom the goods previously belonged, or the limited real rights that burden them.

Part III. Acquisition of Property Rights

217. The ways of acquisition of real rights in the Spanish law are foreseen in Article 609 CC, which refers to occupancy, law, donation, inheritance (with or without testament), certain contracts, followed by the delivery of the goods, and acquisitive prescription.

All of the ways are mechanisms that allow the acquisition of both property and limited real rights upon movable and immovable goods, with the exception of occupancy, which is applied only to the acquisition of property right and is also valid only for movables. These mechanisms may be divided into derivative and original ways of acquisition, depending on the acquisition produced by virtue of the alienation of the right by a previous holder (i.e., donation, contract, and inheritance), or without any link to a previous holder (i.e., occupancy, acquisitive prescription, and acquisition by law).

Chapter 1. Transfer of Property by Contract *Inter Vivos*

218. Article 609 CC contemplates the donation, among the rest of contracts *inter vivos*, as a different way to achieve the acquisition of property and other real rights. This is due to the dual nature of the donation within the Spanish CC, in part as a contract and in part as an institution linked to the donor's inheritance.

The donation is defined in Article 618 CC as a liberal act by which a person disposes, gratuitously, of an object for the benefit of another person, who accepts it. The 'other contracts' alluded to by Article 609 CC concern all the rest whose purpose is the alienation of goods, or the constitution of limited real rights upon them (i.e., sale, exchange, contribution of goods to a company, and transaction). Unlike donation, it is necessary that all these contracts be followed by the delivery of the goods that are the object of the contract (*traditio*) in order to produce the acquisitive effect.

§1. Donation

219. Donation is a contract *inter vivos* whose aim consists of the gratuitous alienation of goods or rights. The one who does the attribution is called 'donor', and the attribution's recipient is called 'donee'. From the donee's perspective, the donation is a way of acquiring the property or any other real right upon an object that has direct and immediate efficacy, contrary to other alienation contracts provided by the CC.

As will be seen below (*infra* §2), in Spanish law, the contractual alienation of property and other real rights is not only required to be based on a 'title', that is, a contract – or other type of juridical act – that is adequate to produce the alienation effect (i.e., sale, exchange), but it also requires the 'conveyance way' or delivery of the goods that are the object of the contract (*traditio*) for the acquisition to be completed. However, in the case of donation, things happen in a different way, because the completion of the contract (i.e., the union of donor's consent and donee's acceptance) produces per se the acquisition of the donated thing or right, without need of *traditio*.[130]

220. The donation's object may consist of both movable and immovable goods, provided that they are already existent at the time the contract is signed (*see* Article 635. I CC, that forbids the donation of future goods).

221. Although the principle of freedom of form in the matter of contracts applies in Spanish law, this general rule presents some exceptions, where it is required that the contract be put into proper form as a validity requirement (contractual form *ad substantiam*). The donation of immovable goods is one of those exceptions. That is because, given its gratuitous character, the donation is a juridical act that could

130. *See* STS 25 Oct. 1993 (*RJA* 1993, 7654).

objectively be prejudicial to a number of people (i.e., donor's inheritors), which explains why the lawmaker has enclosed the donation within some cautions.

Article 633 CC says that for the donation of an immovable to be valid, it must be stated in a notarial deed. The donation (of an immovable) would be void if stated orally or in a private writing. For the donation of movables, Article 632 CC indicates that it could be stated orally or in a private writing, although in the first case, for it to produce effects, the simultaneous delivery of the donated object is required.

222. The donation transfers the property (or the real right at issue) to the donee automatically, without need of previous delivery of the goods. After the completion of the donation – that is to say, after the donee's acceptance – the donation becomes irrevocable, except in some exceptional cases foreseen by the CC in Articles 644–648. These cases are as follows: A son is born to the donor after the donation is made; a donor's son, supposed to be dead, is discovered to be alive after the donation is made; donee's non-fulfilment of burdens; and donee's ingratitude.

§2. Other Contracts *Inter Vivos*

223. Apart from donation, Article 609 CC mentions the completion of 'certain contracts by means of the delivery (of the object being the object of the contract)', among the ways of acquiring property or other real rights.[131]

Unlike Italian and French Law, the Spanish system of contractual acquisition of property is not merely consensual but requires the addition of two elements: 'acquisition title' and 'conveyance way'. 'Acquisition title' or simply 'title' must be understood as a contract able to transfer the property or other real right (i.e., sale, exchange, contribution of goods to a company, and transaction).[132] The 'conveyance way' is the delivery or *traditio* of the goods (which are the object of the contract) to the transferee.

Both elements are equally indispensable within the acquisition of property and limited real rights system. The *acquisition title without the conveyance way* produces only obligatory effects between the parties, which means that the transferee will have merely a personal action to demand the delivery of the goods but that he/she will still not have acquired the property or real right at issue, although the contract has been completed with validity and even in the case where he/she has already performed his/her contractual duties. The *conveyance way without acquisition title* that justifies the transfer of the possession does not have alienation effects either.[133]

---

131. This delivery is the so-called *traditio*.
132. Obviously, the contract must fulfil the general validity requirements: (a) the 'mutual consent', freely expressed, that is to say, provided that both contracting parties are legally qualified and have not suffered from lack of information able to vitiate the contract; (b) a 'determined object', whose traffic is not forbidden; (c) and a 'licit cause', in other words, an economic purpose legally admitted.
133. If the delivery is not based on a previous contract allowing the transfer of the property upon the good, one will be ahead of a payment not due, which will give place to an obligation of restitution on the part of the person who has unduly received the payment (Arts 1895–1901 CC).

224. Legal treatment of the 'conveyance way' or *traditio* cannot be found in the CC, although legal treatment of the delivery obligation (of the sold goods) established within the set of rules referred to in the sale contract usually develops to fill the void.

Article 1462.I CC states that it will be understood that the object sold has been delivered 'when it has been put under the power and possession of the buyer'. To this material delivery are assimilated other forms of *traditio* foreseen in the CC of Spain that can be called 'spiritualized', and as such, the Spanish system approaches the consensualism typical of other legal systems, for example, the French or the Italian ones. One is speaking of the kinds of delivery called 'symbolic', 'consensual', and 'instrumental'.

In the first one, the delivery of the object upon which the property is intended to be transferred ('main object') is made by means of putting another object ('accessory object') that symbolizes or represents the first at the disposal of the transferee. Article 1463 CC contemplates such a type of delivery when it foresees that the alienation of movable goods may be made through the delivery of 'the keys of the places where they are stored or kept'.

The term *consensual delivery* refers to the cases in which the pure agreement of the parties produces by itself an effect that is made legally equivalent to the delivery. This possibility is applied when the object sold cannot be moved into the buyer's power at the time the sale is completed or when the buyer already has the sold object under his/her power, because of any title (different from ownership) previously acquired (*traditio brevi manu*).[134]

Although it is not expressly foreseen in the CC, scholars have admitted that the pure agreement may be equivalent to a material delivery when the conveyor is going to continue having possession of the object after the alienation is made, but in a concept different from the owner, for example, as lessee (*constitutum possessorium*).

Finally, *instrumental delivery* is understood to mean the delivery made through the granting of a notarial deed in which the alienation is stated, unless a contrary will of the parties can be inferred from the document itself (*see* Articles 1462.II and 1464 CC).

225. Although Article 609 CC does not mention it, in order to get the acquisition of property or other real right, a third element is also required: the conveyor being the true holder of the goods or the right transferred and he/she having enough disposition power over it.[135]

Therefore, the one who intends to transfer to another person the property upon an object must hold the ownership of it. The conveyor's lack of ownership, although it does not make the alienation title void, constitutes an impediment for the acquisition of the right, because nobody may transfer something that he/she does not hold (*nemo plus iura ad alium transferre potest quam ipse habet*).

134. *See* STS 31 Oct. 1983 (*RJA* 1983, 5852) STS 20 May 1994 (*RJA* 1994, 3530).

135. This requirement is inferred from other legal provisions, for example, Art. 1950 CC, that when referring to good faith as a requisite to completing an ordinary acquisitive prescription, such a requisite is defined as 'the belief that the person who made the delivery of the object was its owner and was able to transfer his/her ownership'.

The purely *inter partes* efficacy that contracts have, as a general rule, in Spanish law, justifies that the goods (object of the contract) belonging to a person other than the transferrer do not make the contract void: Among other obligations, the conveyor will assume the obligation of acquiring the goods from the hands of their owner, as well as delivering them afterwards to the transferee.

Only if the conveyor is the holder of the transferred goods/right may the transferee complete the acquisition, being in the opposite situation exposed to the exercise of a *vindicatio* by the *verus dominus*. Obviously, this action cannot be successful if the transferee has acquired the right by acquisitive prescription or if the circumstances that exceptionally allow the acquisition *a non domino* should happen.[136]

An obstacle analogous to the conveyor's lack of title is the fact that, related to his/her right, although it effectively belongs to him/her, there is a prohibition to alienate, which impedes him/her the free exercise of the *ius disponendi*. In these circumstances, if the owner alienates the goods/right, the acquisition will not take effect. It would at most be possible that the alienation is mended by alternative mechanisms such as the acquisitive prescription or the acquisition *a non domino*.

136. Both acquisitive prescription and acquisition *a non domino* will be referred to again *infra* Ch. 3.

Chapter 2. Transfer of Property by Death

226. The acquisition of property and other real rights may take place by means of inheritance, which is a way of acquisition based on the alienation of the goods and rights belonging to a deceased person in favour of his/her inheritors. The succession by death may have testamentary or intestate nature. In the first case, the deceased freely appoints his/her heirs through a unilateral juridical act called 'will' or 'testament' or through a successory agreement *inter vivos*.[137] In the second case, provided the deceased did not make a will, the inheritors are appointed by the law.[138]

227. The will is the juridical act used for a person to dispose, for the period after his/her death, of all of his/her properties or a part of them. It is an act: *unilateral*, because only wishes of the testator can be found in it; *inherent to person*, given the fact that it cannot be made by a representative; *formal*, because it must be made according to the solemnities foreseen by law; *revocable* because at any moment up until his/her death the will may be modified; and, obviously, with efficacy *post mortem*.

228. The testator is not fully free when disposing of his/her properties by testament, because the law intends to guarantee that at least a part of his/her goods remains with his/her close family. There is a portion of goods that the testator may not freely transfer because the law has reserved it to determined heirs, who because of this reason are called 'compulsory heirs'.[139] These compulsory heirs are in Spanish Law, first, the sons/daughters or other descendants with regard to their parents or grandparents. Lacking descendants, the deceased's parents or grandparents are compulsory inheritors. In the first case, the extent of this compulsory right reaches two-thirds of the total amount of the inheritance, and it reaches only half of the total amount of the inheritance in the second case.

Moreover, the widow or widower also has a compulsory right to the inheritance. This right, that takes the form of a usufruct, is regardless of the fact that the widow or widower is appointed to the inheritance, together with the deceased's sons/daughters or other descendants or else with the deceased's parents or grandparents. Likewise, the widow's or widower's compulsory right varies depending on the fact of whether she/he has been appointed to the inheritance together with descendants, ascendants, or strangers. In the first case, it consists in the usufruct of a third part of the total amount of the inheritance; in the second case the usufruct will fall upon a half of the total amount of the inheritance, and in the last case, it will reach two-thirds of the total amount of the inheritance.

---

137. This option is very limited within the Spanish CC system because contracts having as their object a person's future inheritance are in general forbidden (Art. 1271 CC). Nevertheless, it is true that some exceptions to this rule can be easily found (e.g., Arts 826, 827 and 1341 CC).
138. Someone's heirs *ab intestato*, according to a priority and excluding order (Arts 930–958 CC) are (1) sons/daughters and other descendants; (2) parents and other ascendants; (3) the widow or widower; and (4) the collateral relatives within the fourth degree. If non-existent, the State appears as the subsidiary legal heir.
139. This portion is known by the name of '*legítima*'.

229. In the matter of succession by death, the Spanish Law follows the Roman Law system, according to which the acquisition of the deceased's goods or rights takes place with the acceptance of the inheritance made by the heir, using the term *stricto sensu*, that is to say, meaning a person who receives entirely the deceased's patrimony or a share of it.[140]

The CC foresees no deadline for the heirs to accept the inheritance, but any interested party (e.g., creditors) may request the judge to define a deadline, not shorter than thirty days, in which every heir must express his/her decision, the inheritance understood to be accepted if the heir does not express a relinquishment.

After the inheritance is accepted, the heir acquires the title to the deceased's goods, rights, and obligations, with retroactive effects up to the moment of death (Article 989 CC). But when there is more than one heir, a joint ownership of the inheritance will be created, within which every heir will hold a share that may be transferred or encumbered in favour of third parties. In these cases, it is necessary to wait for the division of the joint ownership, before the heirs may acquire the ownership upon the specific properties of the inheritance.

230. Unlike the heirs, the beneficiaries of a legacy are not 'universal successors', because they acquire only the deceased's specific goods or rights. They are not responsible for the deceased's debts, neither with their own goods nor with the goods received from the inheritance. If the legacy's object, as is usual, consists of a testator's specific and determined good, then its beneficiary will acquire the ownership only at the time that the inheritance is opened, without need of acceptance (Article 822 CC). Because of that, it has been said, referring to the acquisition of goods or rights that have been the object of a legacy, that the Spanish law takes in, exceptionally, the German system of inheritance acquisition, according to which the transfer occurs *ipso iure* with the death of the person. However, at least for other types of legacies, scholars tend to decide that the legatee's acceptance is necessary.[141]

140. This kind of succession is called 'universal succession', and the heirs *stricto sensu* are, for this reason, 'universal successors'.

141. *See*, for instance, L. Díez-Picazo & A. Gullón, *Sistema de Derecho Civil v. Derecho de Familia: Derecho de Sucesiones* 431–432 (Tecnos 1997).

Chapter 3. Possession

§1. Acquisitive Prescription

231. The acquisitive prescription – or usucapion – is a way of acquiring property and other real rights, based on the undisturbed and non-interrupted possession of an object for a certain length of time as established by law and exercised by a person apart from the owner or holder of a limited real right. The acquisition of the right is the other side of the coin of the loss of that same right to its previous owner, who does not lose his action to claim the property, as the prescription has not been consummated (*see* STS 19 November 2012 (*RJA* 2013, 1246), that overrules the doctrine of the STS 29 April 1987 (*RJA* 1987, 2731)).

The possession that permits the acquisition of the goods or right by means of prescription must be 'by way of owner', 'public', 'undisturbed', and 'non-interrupted'. To possess 'by way of owner' means that the possessor must behave like the true owner or holder; in other words, he/she must do so in a way that externally shows the purpose of holding the goods as his/her owner. It is not that the possessor (necessarily) believes the goods or right is his/hers but only that he/she behaves as if they were so. The possession *ad usucapionem* must also be 'public'; that is, it must be visibly exercised in front of third parties. With this requirement it is intended that the owner of the goods may react against the possession shown by the possessor; and avoid that the period of time necessary to vest the right in this latter is completed.

To be able to produce the usucapion, the possession must also be 'undisturbed', which excludes that one that is reached and maintained by force. Finally, the possession must be 'non-interrupted'. Article 1944 CC says that the possession is interrupted when 'by any cause it is suspended for more than a year'. The interruption is produced also when the owner sues judicially the possessor and he/she is summoned before the court or when the possessor's behaviour shows an express or tacit recognition of the owner's right.

232. Acquisitive prescription can be ordinary or extraordinary. The former's completion requires the possessor being in good faith and having a just title, although this kind of prescription allows the vesting of the (possessed) right in the transferee within a shorter deadline. The extraordinary usucapion requires only the possession, without the need of good faith or just title, but the acquisitive effect takes appreciably more time.

233. What should be understood by 'just title' and 'good faith', with the object of completing an ordinary usucapion?

Just title should be understood as a contract allowing the transfer of property or any other limited real right, that is to say, on the basis of an ordinary usucapion, there must be a contractual title that a priori is adequate to allow the acquisition. It is only the lack of transferor's ownership that impedes the acquisitive effect. According to the STS 10 February 2006 (*RJA* 2006, 1700), the just title may be a revocable, rescindable, or relatively null one. By means of this kind of prescription, the one who has acquired goods from a non-owner may consolidate the (acquired) right due to a lengthy period of possession.

Apart from the just title, the ordinary usucapion also requires the possessor to act in good faith. The good faith, in this context, means the possessor's belief that the transferor of the goods/right is the owner/holder of them and that he/she is legitimated to transfer the property/right at issue.

The periods, for the ordinary prescription, vary according to the nature of the goods that are the object of possession. When these are movable goods, a possession period of three years is required. For immovable goods, a minimum period of ten years is needed, a period that may be prolonged if the owner resides outside Spain.

234. The extraordinary prescription is completed when someone performs a possession by the way of owner, public, undisturbed, and non-interrupted for the period established by law, without need of good faith or just title. The periods for the extraordinary usucapion are considerably longer: six years for movable goods and thirty years for immovable ones, whether the owner does or does not reside in Spain.

§2. Acquisition a *Non Domino*

235. The Spanish law foresees two cases of acquisition *a non domino* in Articles 464 CC and 34 LH, respectively, referred to as movable and immovable goods.[142] The goal of both legal provisions is to protect the third party who believed that the person who transferred the object to him/her was its true owner because of certain external signs that made presumable his/her ownership. The protectable appearance comes from the possession's publicity in the case of movable goods (Article 464 CC)[143] and from the Land Registry's publicity in the case of immovable goods (Article 34 LH). The protection results in impeding that, given certain conditions, a recovery action brought by the actual owner (*verus dominus*) against the third party may succeed.[144]

142. There are no doubts regarding the second of these two legal provisions, but some scholars deny that Art. 464 CC foresees an actual case of acquisition *a non domino*. However, the Courts have interpreted that Art. 464 CC really foresees a case of acquisition *a non domino*. *See* STS 18 Jun. 1930 (*RJA* 1930, 1025), STS 3 Mar. 1980 (*RJA* 1980, 841), and STS 25 Feb. 1992 (*RJA* 1992, 1549).

143. The principle (foreseen in Art. 464 CC) of protection of the third party who onerously and in good faith acquires a chattel is not applicable when this chattel is subjected to a special publicity system, such as the one that is implemented through the Registry of Movables (*see supra* Part II).

144. Despite this, Art. 464 CC permits the actual owner to demand the return of the object, in the case where it had gone out of his/her power because of loss or illegal deprivation.

His/her acquisition, despite being *a non domino*, is automatically produced provided that he/she fulfils some requirements (stated in the mentioned legal provisions), basically: having an onerous title and being in good faith. The automatic character of the acquisition is the main difference if compared with the ordinary usucapion, which allows the vesting the right in the transferee only after a period of possession established by law.

Chapter 4. Accession

236. According to Article 353 CC, the property on goods gives right, by accession, to all that persons produce or all that comes to be joined or incorporated to them, naturally or artificially. In the first case, one speaks of 'discrete' accession (in the sense of a countable increase of the goods), and in the second one of 'continuous' accession (in the sense of an uncountable growth of the goods). In the discrete accession, one assists in a fructification phenomenon that originates a new object, separated from the productive one (*res frugifera*), and in the continuous accession, one finds a way to acquire something that operates when an object (called 'accessory' object) is incorporated into another ('principal' or 'main' object) in an indissoluble way, that is to say, in such a manner that the former cannot be detached without causing damage to the latter. It can be said that in the continuous accession, there is a physical extension of the goods that are the object of the right, although in the discrete accession, there is a multiplication of the goods into smaller ones (the 'fruits').

Nevertheless, when the accession *stricto sensu* is mentioned as a way to acquire property or other limited real rights, scholars and jurisprudence are really referring only to the continuous accession. The same will be done in this chapter.

237. The (continuous) accession is based on a general principle that is usually designed with the Latin expression *accesorium sequitur principale*, according to which, when a permanent incorporation of an accessory object to a principal one happens, the owner of the principal object makes his/hers the accessory one by accession. Obviously, this effect is true regardless of the obligation to compensate the accessory object's owner, depending on the circumstances of the incorporation (Article 358 CC).

Within the continuous accession, several species should be distinguished because some cases of incorporation are due to natural forces ('natural accession') and others to human activity ('industrial accession'). However, as the basis for this classification, the criterion of the nature (immovable or movable) of the goods affected by the union or incorporation of others will be used here. The CC devotes Articles 358–374 to the immovable accession and to the movable accession Articles 375–383.

§1. Immovable Accession

238. The owner of the ground or land on which a third party has built, planted, or sown will have the right to make his/hers the work, planting or crops sown, compensating the necessary expenses to the person who made any of them and provided that this person acted in good faith. This is a specific application of the principle *accesorium sequitur principale*, known as *superficies solo cedit.* In addition to this first option, the owner of the ground also has the opposite option, that is, to oblige the one who built or planted to keep the ground for him/her, in exchange for the corresponding price, or to oblige the one who sows the crops to pay a mandatory lease rent proportional to the time the ground was used.

The CC does not foresee the case of extra-limited constructions (i.e., the ones that are made mainly on one's own ground and only in a small part on another person's ground), but when something like this occurs, the Courts have shown in favour of applying the theory of the 'reverse accession', according to which, when the construction has more value than the portion of invaded ground, the principle *superficie solo cedit* must be reversed, with the result that the building comes to be the principal object and the ground the accessory one.[145]

239. When the planting, the construction, or the crops sown are carried out on someone's own ground but by using another person's materials, the materials' owner may remove them as long as this action does not cause any damage to the planting, the construction, or the crops sown. If this is not the case, the ground's owner may acquire the materials, compensating the materials' owner with their value and, when there has been bad faith, compensating (if caused) for the damages as well (Article 360 CC).

240. The CC regulates several cases of immovable natural accession, in the major part caused by the force of fluvial waters. One of them is the case known as 'alluvion', that is, produced by the slowly formed alluvium of materials from highlands to lowlands by virtue of the rivers' current. On this issue, Article 366 CC states that 'the increase that these lands adjacent to the rivers' banks gradually receive by effect of the waters' current belongs to the owners of these lands'.

§2. Movable Accession

241. A first case of movable accession is the 'adjunction', which consists of the inseparable joining of two or more heterogeneous movable goods that belong to different owners. Article 375 resolves the conflict generated by the 'adjunction' applying the principle *accesorium sequitur principale* and giving several criteria to decide, among two or more adjunct objects, which of them should be considered principal and which of them accessory.

First of all, the accessory relationship is determined in view of the destiny of the objects at issue in such a manner that the object that is joined to another for purpose of decoration, use, or perfection (Article 376 CC, *sensu contrario*) is qualified as accessory. If it cannot be determined according to the previous rule which among the objects is the principal one, the object with the highest value (Article 377 CC) will be considered as such. If all the objects have equivalent value, or their value cannot be determined, the object with the largest size will be considered as principal (Article 377 CC).

242. Second, another case of movable accession is the 'mixture'. Unlike adjunction, the mixture produces an indissoluble union of homogeneous objects, which are all jumbled together, totally losing their individuality. If the mixture is made by

145. *See* STS 12 Nov. 1985 (*RJA* 1985, 5582) and STS 29 Jul. 1994 (*RJA* 1994, 6305).

chance or by will of the (two or more) owners of the mixed objects, each owner will be vested a quota of property proportional to the respective value of his/her object (Article 381 CC).

The same solution applies when the mixture has been produced by will of one of the owners at issue acting in good faith (Article 382 CC). However, if the mixture has been made by one of the owners at issue acting in bad faith, the responsible one will lose any right to the outcome, and he/she will be obliged to compensate the owner(s) of the other mixed object(s) because of the damages (if they exist) (Article 382 CC).

243. Finally, it is necessary to mention the *specificatio*, understood as the making of a new article out of someone's chattel by means of another person's labour. Although it is included among the legal provisions on accession, the *specificatio* causes no incorporation, nor does it speak of a principal object or an accessory one. What exists in this case is only the application of personal work on another person's chattel. Article 383 CC resolves the conflict between the work's maker and the chattel's owner, depending on the former acting in good or bad faith.

When the one who has made the *specificatio* has acted in good faith, he/she may make the work his/hers, compensating its owner for the chattel's value (Article 383.I CC). However, if the chattel's value is higher than the cost of the work, it is the owner who has the option of either keeping the new species after compensating the maker for the cost of the work or asking for the compensation of the chattel's value (Article 383.II CC).

When the one who has made the *specificatio* has acted in bad faith, the chattel's owner may either make the new species his/hers without paying the maker for the cost of the work or demand that the maker pay compensation for the chattel's value and the damages caused to him/her (Article 383.III CC).

Chapter 5. Occupancy

244. The occupancy is a way to acquire property (i.e., it is not suitable for limited real rights) that is based on the possessory taking or appropriation of goods without an owner (*res nullius* or *res derelicta*), with the purpose of having them as owner. It is regulated in Articles 610–617 CC. By means of occupancy, it is possible to acquire ownership only of corporeal movables. Article 610 CC, after indicating that occupancy is applicable for 'goods liable to appropriation by its nature' as well as 'for the lack of an owner', exemplifies such category of goods as animals being the object of hunting and fishing,[146] treasures,[147] and derelict movable goods.

245. When referring to 'goods liable to appropriation by its nature', all those goods whose traffic is forbidden are excluded. Also immovable goods are excluded, especially if one notes that Article 17 Law on Public Administration Patrimony (LPAP) vests *ope legis* in the State the ownership of all the immovable goods that are derelict, which includes all those without a known owner.

As regards the requirement that the goods liable to occupancy must be goods 'without owner', it may be fulfilled because the goods have never had such an owner (*res nullius* by nature) or because they have been abandoned by their owner (*res derelicta*).

Therefore, the goods are not liable to occupancy if, although they are not under the possession of anyone, it can be understood that they do belong to someone, either because they are not the kind of goods that are *nullius* by nature or because it cannot be rationally supposed that anybody has abandoned them. The finder, in the case of possessory taking of this kind of goods (lost goods, in sum), is not allowed to acquire their ownership but obliged to fulfil the return obligations foreseen in Article 615 CC. This legal provision states that the finder must try to return the found object to its owner or, if impossible, to deliver it to the mayor of the area where the object has been found.

If the owner has not made an appearance to reclaim his/her property two years after the property was handed in, the finder may make the object (or its price, if it had been necessary to sell it in order to avoid its waste) his/hers. Conversely, if the owner appears to reclaim the object found within that biennial period, the finder will have the right to receive a reward equivalent to the tenth part of the object's value (Article 616 CC).

146. Only wild animals can be the object of hunting and fishing, provided that these activities are fulfilled according to the special laws that regulate them. Currently, the great majority of these special laws on hunting and fishing are laws passed by the CC AA, insofar as Art. 148.1.11 CE gives the power to them to make laws on this issue, with the exception of deep-sea fishing. Nevertheless, the old state Laws on hunting (4 Apr. 1970) and river fishing (20 Feb. 1942) are still in force, whose content would be applicable for lack of legal provision on the matter passed by an autonomic parliament.

147. The 'treasure' is defined, for legal purposes, as a hidden and unknown deposit of money, jewellery, or other precious objects, whose ownership is not stated (Art. 352 CC). According to Art. 351 CC, the treasure belongs to the owner of the estate on which the treasure has been found. However, if the finding happened by chance, due to a person other than the land's owner, the treasure will belong by halves to the finder together with the estate's owner.

Chapter 6. Expropriation

246. The expropriation is a way to transfer a right of property by means of the deprivation of the goods being the object of the right, compulsorily decided by the appropriate administrative department. The expropriation must be justified because of a public utility or a social interest, and it requires the owner who suffers it to be paid an appraisal in exchange for the object of expropriation (Article 349.I CC and Article 33.3 CE). The goods/rights expropriated are acquired by the expropriating department or by a different organization as beneficiary of the expropriation.

The regulation on the procedure for carrying out expropriation is contained in the Law on Mandatory Expropriation (16 December 1954 (LEF)). A previous declaration of public utility, stated in a Law passed by the Cortes Generales, is required. Nevertheless, this declaration is considered to be implicit when the (immovable) goods are included either in a project of construction or in an urban development plan.[148] When this declaration is made, the Administration will decide on the need of taking the concrete goods and acquiring the rights indispensable for the expropriation's goals. The record of goods/rights affected by the procedure must be published in the State Official Gazette, at least when the expropriation is carried out by a State body. It is intended with this publicity that anybody may oppose the planned expropriation, expressing the reasons for considering as a preferring option the expropriation of other goods/rights other than the ones included in the record. In view of these reasons, it will be decided, if pertinent, a resolution, on the need of taking, liable to appeal at the request of the affected party. With this resolution the expropriation procedure is properly started.

First of all, the appraisal to be paid by the expropriating Administration to the good's owner will be determined. The estimate may be done through an agreement made (between the owner and the Administration) within the deadline foreseen in the LEF. But if no agreement is reached within that term, an arbitration administrative organization (called Province Expropriation Jury) must then intervene. This body, composed of members legally designed, is chaired by a Magistrate, who must take into account the allegations of all the affected parties. The Jury must make a decision by majority and this decision must be notified to the owner and the expropriating Administration, who may oppose it by means of a judicial appeal.

After the appraisal has been determined, the expropriating Administration is obliged to make payment within a term of six months. After paying the appraisal, the goods may be the object of a possessory taking by the expropriating Administration or the beneficiary of the expropriation. Besides this ordinary procedure of expropriation, the LEF foresees an exceptional urgent procedure that gives place to the possessory taking of the good before the payment of the appraisal has been made.

148. On the development planning, *see supra* Part I, paras 96–101.

Chapter 7. Insolvency

247. This subject is not applicable in Spanish Law.

Chapter 8. Acquisition *Ministerio Legis*

248. There are many cases of acquisition *ministerio legis* stated in the Spanish legal order. With a general character, they are foreseen in Article 609 CC, which mentions the 'law' being one of the possible ways of acquisition of property and other limited real rights.

Among others, the case regulated in Article 17 LPAP can be mentioned. That article says that the State must automatically be vested in the ownership with all immovable goods without an owner. Another example would be the acquisition that occurs in the bosom of the kind of marriage partnership that accords each spouse to be automatically vested in the ownership of half of the earnings obtained by the other (*see* Articles 1344 et seq. CC).

Part IV. Trust and Fiduciary Mechanisms

Introduction

249. As stated above (*see* General Introduction), although the institution of trust is unknown in Spanish Law, some other institutions of fiduciary nature that can fulfil a function very similar to the trust's one are admitted in our legal order. Nevertheless, there are noticeable differences between trust and those other fiduciary mechanisms. These differences can be shown in the following points:[149]

(a) In Spanish Law, it is very difficult to accept the existence of two simultaneous titles of property in the same goods, all of them with ability to obtain autonomous judicial protection (as it occurs in the Anglo-American trust with the trustee's legal ownership and the beneficiary's equity ownership).
(b) Although the Spanish fiduciary mechanisms require being constituted in a formal way, by means of an express declaration of will, either *inter vivos* or *mortis causa*, the Anglo-American trust admits several ways of constitution. On the one hand, there are the trusts constituted on the basis of an express declaration of will, whether *inter vivos* or *mortis causa* (express trusts). On the other hand, there are the trusts deduced from the presumable will of someone who conveys/acquires goods under determined circumstances (resulting trusts) or automatically derived from a legal provision (constructive trusts).
(c) The Anglo-American trust fulfils a greater number of functions than the traditional fiduciary mechanisms in Civil Law countries because it is not only useful to get the administration of an inheritance or a familial patrimony, or to endow some goods with a guarantee aim, but also to attend to some social interest purposes, to manage securities or immovable goods under a time-sharing regime, or to get a representation quota in the bosom of a company with the object of vote. In spite of everything, the legal orders of Civil Law countries show a recent trend to incorporate fiduciary mechanisms directed to fulfil some of those same functions. Particularly in the field of investment and management of securities, given that the trust was shown to be a useful instrument, Civil Law countries have incorporated systems of fiduciary management of securities and funds very similar to some kinds of trust (*see infra* Chapter 1, §2. II).[150]

149. *See* S. Cámara Lapuente, *Operaciones fiduciarias o trusts en Derecho español, Revista Crítica de Derecho Inmobiliario,* 1763–1764 (September–October 1999).
150. *See* M. Checa Martínez, *El trust angloamericano en el Derecho español* 17 (McGraw Hill 1998).

(d) Unlike what happens in Civil Law countries, trust is an institution in which, despite its private law character, the judicial powers of intervention are very large, to the extent that the judge can substitute the trustee if he/she resigns or misuses his/her powers.

250. In Spanish Law, it is usual to refer to, on the one hand, fiduciary mechanisms *inter vivos*, which at the same time may have an aim of management (*fiducia cum amico*) or an aim of guarantee (*fiducia cum creditore*),[151] and, on the other hand, fiduciary mechanisms *mortis causa*, some of them possibly coming from the will of the testator and others directly foreseen by a legal provision (more or less, like the Anglo-American constructive trusts are).[152]

The fiduciary mechanisms *mortis causa* are always directed to an aim of management, but unlike the major part of cases of *fiducia cum amico* agreed *inter vivos*, they are not foreseen in favour of the person who has set them up but in favour of a third party who is the beneficiary of the patrimony temporarily put in the hands of the fiduciary.

251. With regard to the fiduciary mechanisms *inter vivos*, it has to be known that, despite there being no statutory provisions on it, its validity and legal regime are set up by the jurisprudence on the basis of the principle of 'autonomy of the will' or, in other words, individual freedom of contract (Article 1255 CC). In some TS cases, it can be read that 'it (the fiduciary contract *inter vivos*) lies in a patrimonial grant that one contracting party, called the settlor,[153] makes in favour of the other one, called the fiduciary, for this latter to use that patrimonial mass with an agreed aim, and provided that, when the foreseen aim is accomplished, the fiduciary must convey again the patrimonial mass object of the contract to a third party (beneficiary)'.[154]

The fiduciary mechanism *inter vivos* has been traditionally defined as the complex result from the combination of two simple juridical acts or, in other words, as a juridical act that produces a duplicity of legal effects ('double-effect theory'): a first effect, in the field of property rights, by virtue of which the settlor transfers fully and irreversibly to the fiduciary the property upon the object of the contract; and a second one, in the field of obligations and rights of credit, by means of which the fiduciary assumes the obligation to apply the object to a determined aim, as well as to return it later to the settlor himself/herself or to a third party. According to this

151. These fiduciary mechanisms *inter vivos* have constantly been the subject of controversy either among scholars or among courts.
152. By virtue of a legal provision, certain legal duties arise as well, which in the context of a deal *inter privatos* means a sort of *fiducia cum amico* (in Spanish Law, these cases are often being referred to as the concept of 'legal obligations'). It occurs, for example, with the seller's obligation to preserve the sold goods exactly in the same state as they were at the time of the sale, until the moment when the delivery happens (Art. 1468.I CC). Some of these cases are clearly corresponding with some of the cases that in English Law give rise to a constructive trust.
153. We have opted to use the term *settlor* to refer to the *fiducia*'s constituent person, although this term is peculiar to Anglo-American trust. In Spanish, this person would be called '*fiduciante*'.
154. *See* STS 2 Dec. 1996 (*RJA* 1996, 8784) and STS 4 Jul. 1998 (*RJA* 1998, 5413).

explanation, if the fiduciary does not fulfil his/her obligations, the settlor has only a personal action in order to demand compensation from the fiduciary for damages.

The double-effect theory currently does not have many followers, neither among scholars nor among courts. The main criticism of it has been based on the consideration that the Spanish system of contracts is characterized by the requirement of a cause for every contract, therefore, abstract juridical acts not being accepted. Consequently, it is not possible to admit that a contract based on a *causa fiduciae* permits the transfer of a property right. On the contrary, currently the most accepted theory is the one that says that, in this kind of juridical act, an authentic conveyance of property in favour of the fiduciary does not happen, but he/she receives only an apparent or merely functional title.

The fiduciary's apparent title would serve to protect the hypothetical third party who acquired, onerously and in good faith, one or more goods being part of the object of the fiduciary act, but it would not be enough to avoid that, in case of illicit use or conveyance of one or more of those goods, the settlor demanding one or more of the goods from the hands of the fiduciary or the hypothetical third party who had acquired it/them gratuitously or in bad faith. In short, the third parties will be protected against the settlor's recovery action when, in accordance with the provisions relative to the acquisitions *a non domino*, they must be maintained in their rights.[155] Therefore, according to this theory, the goods being the object of the fiduciary juridical act do not belong to the fiduciary's private patrimony, in such a manner that, in case of the fiduciary's bankruptcy, the settlor has the power to demand that these goods are not included among the fiduciary's assets, and, in case of the settlor's bankruptcy, his/her creditors may demand these goods to be reintegrated with the rest of their debtor's assets.

252. The various cases of *fiducia cum amico* and *fiducia cum creditore* will be examined in Chapters 1 and 2 following the general outlines of the *International Encyclopaedia of Laws*. Nevertheless, it is worth mentioning that the matter relative to fiduciary mechanisms has not had a homogeneous legal treatment all over the Spanish territory. As it has been said above, the CC AA enjoy in Spain a significant degree of political and legal autonomy. Some of them have even the competence to enact Private Law statutes on different matters. Navarre and Catalonia especially stand out, the two territories with a greater self lawmaking tradition. In the field of the *fiducia cum amico* and the *fiducia cum creditore*, both Navarre and Catalonia have special laws whose content does not correspond with that of the CC rules in force within the rest of Spain on this matter. These Catalonian and Navarrese rules will have to be taken into account in order to resolve the legal disputes that arise within the respective territorial scope.

155. On the acquisitions *a non domino*, depending on the movable or immovable nature of the goods at issue, *see supra* paras 89, 213 and 235.

Chapter 1. Administration of Property: *Fiducia Cum Amico*

§1. Introduction

253. One speaks of *fiducia cum amico* when the settlor conveys to the fiduciary an apparent property right upon one or more goods (i.e., a greater or smaller patrimonial mass) for the fiduciary to carry out some kind of management activity regarding it/them. This fiduciary's management activity may lie in the mere custody of the goods, their diligent administration (i.e., obtaining of fruits or rents), or it may even come to imply the goods' alienation in favour of a third party followed by a diligent management of the money received in return. The *fiducia cum amico* is compatible with the fact that the fiduciary receives some kind of payment for its performance, maybe by means of the permission to use the goods given to him/her under a fiduciary title or to obtain the fruits or rents that they produce.

254. The interest to protect can be the settlor's one, to whom the goods fiduciarily transferred (or those acquired instead of them) will have to be returned in the end, or a beneficiary's one, whom the settlor wants to favour, as happens with the successory modalities of *fiducia cum amico.*

255. First, the cases of *fiducia cum amico* that have a contractual origin (*infra* §2.I), paying special attention to those related to the transfer of a fiduciary title with a goal of a movable patrimonial mass' investment and management (*infra* §2.II), will be examined. Second, the scope of the *fiducia cum amico* within the field of the Successory Law (*infra* §3) will be analysed.

§2. *Fiducia Cum Amico* Agreed by Contract *Inter Vivos*

I. In General

256. In the *fiducia cum amico* agreed upon by contract *inter vivos*, it is the contracting parties' mutual consent that gives place to the apparent title that the settlor transfers to the fiduciary. In the *fiducia cum amico* originated by contract, a dichotomy can be found between the contract cause apparently wanted by the contracting parties and the actual purpose followed by them. This dichotomy is apparent through the internal arrangement agreed upon by the contracting parties, normally put in form by means of a detached deed in relation to the transferring contract. In this internal agreement (*pactum fiduciae*), from which the purely apparent character of the fiduciary's title can be inferred, both contracting parties set the obligations that the fiduciary assumes with regard to the settlor.[156]

156. Otherwise, this dichotomy, coming from the combination of an external contractual mechanism and an internal *pactum fiduciae*, is also present in the cases of by-contract originated *fiducia cum creditore*.

257. The normal running of a fiduciary relationship *cum amico* implies the conveyance of an apparent title upon one or more goods, the carrying out of the management that the fiduciary had assumed by means of the internal arrangement agreed upon with the settlor, and the return of the object of the fiduciary operation after the management has been fulfilled (*see* Sentences of the Supreme Court (SSTS) 5 March 2001 (*RJA* 2001, 3972), 31 October 2003 (*RJA* 2003, 7977), 27 July 2006 (*RJA* 2006, 6144)).

The transfer of the fiduciary title upon the goods is not conceived in order to protect the fiduciary's interest, as occurs in the cases of *fiducia cum creditore*, but in order to protect the settlor's one: The management that he/she wants the fiduciary to carry out in favour of him/her can be done in a more appropriate way if he/she transfers the title upon the goods to the fiduciary (e.g., a painter who fiduciarily sells his/her paintings to a merchant or a gallery for them to manage the sale of those paintings).

The fiduciary's title is obviously a temporary one, whose term is determined by the kind of management activity that the fiduciary has assumed.

258. Because of the character that this type of *fiducia* has, particularly because of the aim that, thanks to the *pactum fiduciae*, can be deduced that the contracting parties actually follow, a great number of TS' sentences have stressed the similarity with the typical *inter partes* relation that arises from the contract of mandate (ruled in Articles 1709–1739 CC), especially with the modality in which the mandatary acts without showing to the third parties his/her character of representative from the mandator (Article 1717 CC).[157]

The mandate, such as defined in Article 1709 CC, is a contract by means of which a person (the mandatary) assumes the obligation to carry out a service or to take some step on behalf of another person (the mandatory or the principal). Contracting with third parties, the mandatary may act *proprio nomine*. In this case, Article 1717 CC states that the mandatary will be the sole person obligated with regard to those third parties. It is true that Article 1717 foresees an exception 'if (the object of the contract) was some mandator's own goods', which has been understood by the jurisprudence in the sense of 'goods plainly belonging to the mandator', then, the exception cannot play in *fiducia cum amico* cases because the mandatary-fiduciary has an apparent title upon the goods that are the object of management.

According to the mandate's legal regime, the mandatary, when the management is finished, must account for his/her actions before the principal, included the delivery of all the goods that he/she has received by virtue of the steps taken.[158]

157. *See* STS 4 May 1950 (*RJA* 1950, 732), STS 9 Oct. 1987 (*RJA* 1987, 6769), STS 30 Apr. 1992 (*RJA* 1992, 4474), STS 21 Mar. 1995 (*RJA* 1995, 2051), STS 24 Mar. 1997 (*RJA* 1997, 2477).

158. In the case that gave place to the STS 13 Jul. 2009 (*RJA* 2009, 4466), the fiduciary assignment of a piece of art in order to manage the sale of it to a third party by the fiduciary, was combined with a simulated loan from the fiduciary to the settlor with the product of the sale. The Supreme Court rejects the fiduciary's claim to recovery the sum given through the loan, taking into account that it represented the amount that the fiduciary was obliged to return to the settlor in the frame of their fiduciary relationship.

259. There is an irregular development of the *fiducia cum amico* relationship when the fiduciary does not take all the agreed-upon steps or when he/she does not carry them out with correctness (e.g., he/she applies the object of the agreement in his/her own benefit, or he/she transfers the goods to a third party against the purpose agreed upon with the settlor).[159] An irregularity also occurs when the fiduciary, after taking all the agreed-upon steps correctly, refuses to return the goods to the settlor. Another kind of distortion can arise from the fact that the fiduciary finds himself/herself enveloped within an insolvency process and subjected to the subsequent seizure provoked by his/her creditors.[160]

The non-fulfilment or incorrect fulfilment of the agreed-upon steps will give to the settlor the right to ask for compensation for the damages caused to him/her from the fiduciary. However, the settlor, in his/her condition of actual owner of the goods, may always bring an action in order to retrieve the goods from the fiduciary's hands (*see* STS 27 July 2006 (*RJA* 2006, 6144)). These actions could belong to the beneficiary and not to the settlor, if the fiduciary mechanism has been made to favour a person other than the settlor. The beneficiary, however, can find it difficult to show the existence of a fiduciary agreement in his/her favour and therefore the apparent character of the fiduciary's title.[161] The fiduciary, at most, may assert a retention right upon the goods that are the object of the *fiducia* when, as a consequence of taking the agreed-upon steps, he/she has made some expenses and the settlor has not reimbursed them to him/her (*see* Article 1730 CC, if the fiduciary relationship can be referred to the mandate's scheme, or Article 1780 CC, if it can be referred to the deposit's scheme).[162]

The settlor's action will not be successful when the goods are in the hands of a third party who has acquired them onerously and in good faith from the fiduciary.

In the case of fiduciary's insolvency, the settlor may bring an action in order to avoid the fiduciary's creditors' seizing the goods that are the object of *fiducia*. It would be an action derived from a third party's property right.[163] In the case of the fiduciary's finding himself/herself enveloped in a bankruptcy process, the settlor has the right to impede that the goods that are the object of the *fiducia* are classified as goods belonging to the fiduciary's patrimony. If the bankruptcy process affects the settlor, the fiduciary is obliged to return the goods to the settlor's patrimony.

II. Investment Funds and Pension Funds

260. Investment funds and pension funds are two specific applications of the contractually originated *fiducia cum amico*. They are both methods of saving and security that, as in other countries, are currently implanted in Spain in a very strong

159. *See* STS 27 Feb. 2007 (*RJA* 2007, 1768).

160. *See* S. Cámara Lapuente, *Operaciones fiduciarias o trusts en Derecho español, Revista Crítica de Derecho Inmobiliario*, 1795 (September–October 1999).

161. *See* S. Cámara Lapuente, *Operaciones fiduciarias o trusts en Derecho español, Revista Crítica de Derecho Inmobiliario*, 1813 (September–October 1999).

162. On the retention right as a possible mechanism of guarantee, *see infra* Part V, Ch. 2.

163. On this issue, see *supra* Part I, para. 93.

manner. They are both probably the best examples of adaptation of some aspects of the Anglo-American trust into Civil Law-tradition countries.

261. Investment funds are ruled in Spain through Law 35/2003 (4 November 2003), on Collective Investment Entities. This Law has been developed later through the R.D. 1082/2012 (13 July 2012), subsequently developed through minor rules.

Article 3.1 of this Law defines the investment funds as patrimonies belonging to a plurality of investors, managed by a management company that, without being the fund's owner, has upon it the kind of powers typical for an owner (acquisition, tenancy, enjoyment, management, alienation of the securities, or the financial assets that composed the fund).

Although it is obvious that the title given to investment funds management companies is a fiduciary one, the legal nature of these funds is explained by means of another kind of argument, such as saying that the fund belongs, as a co-ownership, to all the people who take part in it, who give a sort of mandate to manage the fund to the management company, or explaining that the fund constitutes a sort of entity founded on an associative basis regarding every person who integrates the fund as having a participation.

262. As regards pension funds, its legal regime is contained in Legislative Decree 1/2002 (29 November 2002), on Pension Plans and Funds, later developed by R.D. 304/2004 (20 February 2004).

As investment funds, pension funds are patrimonial masses without legal personality that are created due to the contribution of a plurality of people. The pension funds' management, custody, and control are carried out by a specialized entity according to the arrangements agreed upon in a pension plan. The aim of these pension funds and plans is not an investment one, but a security one, in order to secure future needs of the fund's contributors.

On the legal nature of these kinds of funds, the most plausible explanation is again one of a fiduciary contract between the contributors and the fund's management company, and consequently the one of the mere apparent title of the latter one on the patrimonial mass managed by it. Nevertheless, the interpretation according to which the fund belongs as a co-ownership to the contributors, who would make a mandate contract with the society put in charge of the fund's management, has also been proposed, as well as the interpretation that pension funds have a structure similar to that of a company, or even that these funds constitute a *universitas rerum* similar to the patrimony given in order to create a foundation.

§3. *Fiducia Cum Amico* in the Field of Successory Law

I. The Fiduciary Substitution

263. Articles 781 et seq. CC state a kind of hereditary substitution, inspired by the Roman *fideicommissum*, by virtue of which the testator entrusts a first inheritor (the 'fiduciary') with the mission of preserving and subsequently transferring the whole or a part of the inheritance in favour of a second inheritor (the substitute). Actually, more than an assignment entrusted from the testator to the fiduciary, and a subsequent conveyance in favour of the second inheritor, there is a double and successive calling to the inheritance: first, in favour of the fiduciary, and second (after a term is over or a condition has been fulfilled) in favour of the substitute. But both of them inherit from the testator.[164]

264. Using the fiduciary substitution, the testator may make more than a successive calling to the inheritance, in such a manner that an enchantment of several people between the first fiduciary and the (latter) inheritor occurs. People situated in the series between these two have at the same time the status of fiduciary (with regard to those who follow in the series) and substitute (in relation to those who go before). Nevertheless, in order to avoid undesirable perpetual links to property rights, Article 781 CC forbids the testator from making more than two successive callings in favour of people not alive at the time the inheritance is available. On the contrary, there is no limit to successive callings in favour of people already alive at the time of the death of the testator.

265. Although the fiduciary acquires the property upon the rights composing the trusteeship subjected to substitution, this property is a temporary or conditional one because he/she must transfer the trusteeship to the substitute when the term or the condition foreseen by the testator is over or fulfilled. Moreover, he/she must preserve the goods composing the trusteeship in good state, making his/her position very similar to that typical of a usufructuary.

As a result, many legal provisions regarding usufruct are analogically applicable to the fiduciary's status (*see supra* Part I). The substitute may bring an action against the fiduciary who does not fulfil this duty of maintenance correctly. After the fiduciary has transferred the goods composing the trusteeship to the substitute in good state, he/she has a right to be compensated for the costs made relating to the trusteeship's maintenance and improvements.

266. In the modality known as 'residue trusteeship', the fiduciary is authorized to alienate, with greater or less freedom, the goods comprising the object of the trusteeship. His/her duty before the substitute is simply giving to him/her the goods that remain within the trusteeship when the substitution time is over (the 'residue'). The residue trusteeship embraces two different classes: *si aliquid supererit* (the alienation powers given to the fiduciary are so wide that it is not certain there will be any residue for the substitute),[165] and *de eo quod supererit* (the fiduciary may not alienate the whole trusteeship because the testator's will requires some residue be left to the substitute).

164. Because of this fact, it does not matter if the second inheritor should die before the fiduciary; the former's right will be transferred to his/her inheritors.

165. *See* an application of this type of residue trusteeship in STS 7 Nov. 2008 (*RJA* 2008, 7696).

267. If for any reason the substitution becomes invalid, or the substitute is unable to inherit from the testator, the fiduciary will become a pure inheritor (i.e., with no further burdens or duties).

II. The Successory Reserves

268. Spanish CC foresees two types of successory reserves: the 'widow(er) reserve', which is imposed on the widow or widower who remarries, with regard to the goods acquired from her/his dead spouse by means of inheritance or donation, and in favour of the sons, daughters, and other descendants from the first marriage (Articles 968 et seq. CC); and the 'lineage reserve', which obliges the ascendant who has inherited from a descendant goods that the latter had inherited from another ascendant or a brother/sister, to reserve a part of these goods in favour of relatives within the third degree belonging to the lineage from which the goods come (Article 811 CC).

Unlike the fiduciary substitutions, which are created by the testator's will, reserves originate directly in a legal provision. Consequently, one is in the presence of cases of *fiducia cum amico* constituted *ministerio legis.*

269. The person obliged as a result of the reserve does not have a full title upon the goods subjected to it, basically because he/she cannot freely alienate the goods *mortis causa.*[166] After his/her death, the reserved goods will automatically go to the people in favour of whom the reserve was imposed.[167] However, while the reserve lasts, the person obliged as a result of it assumes the duty to preserve in good state the goods being the object of the reserve, and even he/she must take several security measures, such as making an inventory of the goods subjected to the reserve, appraising the movable ones, recording in the Land Registry the condition of 'reserved' of the immovable ones, or mortgaging some other goods to guarantee the value that will have to be paid, if the case arises, to the beneficiaries of the reserve.

270. There is a case that can be compared, to a certain extent, to the successory reserves. We refer to the return of the goods coming from the inheritance of a missing person, who has been declared dead as a result of a judicial process, but happens to be alive and reappears in his/her home.

Although the judicial declaration of someone's death gives rise to opening his/her succession and to dividing his/her inheritance, for a five-year security term, the legacies will not be paid nor will the inheritors be able to convey gratuitously the goods coming from the inheritance (Article 196 CC).

The inheritors of the person judicially declared dead must make an inventory of the goods that compose the inheritance at issue. Nevertheless, they have no duty of preservation with regard to these goods: If the person *de cuius hereditate agitur*

166. He/she retains, however, the power to alienate the goods by means of contracts *inter vivos*, provided that the beneficiaries of the reserve retain the right to receive the value of the goods alienated by the former as well.

167. Obviously, so long they exist at the time when the person obliged to the reserve dies.

reappears, the goods that composed his/her patrimony must be returned to him/her in whatever state they are in. If the goods have been sold, he/she will be paid with the price received or the goods subsequently acquired with this price. The ex-inheritors will not have to pay rents, fruits, or products from the goods that they had obtained from the inheritance for the period between the judicial declaration of death and the reappearance (Article 197 CC).

III. Forbidden Testamentary Provisions

271. Spanish CC forbids testamentary provisions whose aim is to give someone a whole or a part of an inheritance with the goal that he/she applies the goods according to secret instructions given by the testator (Article 785.4 CC). It is also forbidden that the testator's last will be orally communicated to a trustworthy person, who subsequently conveys it as a *nuntius*. Finally, the Anglo-American secret and half-secret trusts are not contemplated in the Spanish legal order.[168]

168. *See* S. Cámara Lapuente, *Operaciones fiduciarias o trusts en Derecho español, Revista Crítica de Derecho Inmobiliario*, 1844–1845 (September–October 1999).

Chapter 2. Security: *Fiducia Cum Creditore*

§1. Fiduciary Juridical Act *Cum Creditore*: General Features

272. One considers a case of *fiducia cum creditore* when the fiduciary is a debtor who transfers to his/her creditor the fiduciary title upon one or more goods with the goal of guaranteeing the debt contracted with the latter (*see also* Parts I, II and V). This means that the fiduciary juridical act with a goal of guarantee has, as protagonists, two persons linked because of a previous credit relationship: The debtor transfers the goods to his/her creditor with an additional agreement in accordance with that the creditor will return the goods to the debtor when the guaranteed debt has been paid.[169]

The fiduciary's title, exactly the same as occurs with the *fiducia cum amico*, is a temporary and functional one. However, unlike the *fiducia cum amico*, in the cases of *fiducia cum creditore* it is not the settlor's interest but the fiduciary's one that comes into play because the fiduciary is the creditor whose credit is intended to guarantee. The title upon the trusted goods, although a fiduciary one, gives the creditor the surety that the goods will not be the object of conveyance on the part of the debtor, in particular that they will not be given as a guarantee in favour of other creditors.

273. In normal conditions, that is to say, if the settlor-debtor pays the guaranteed debt, he/she will be able to bring an action, based on the *pactum fiducia*, in order to obtain the return of the goods. This is a real action because the settlor-debtor never loses the property upon the goods trusted to the fiduciary.

On the contrary, if the settlor-debtor fails to fulfil the debt or does not fulfil it correctly, the fiduciary may lawfully oppose the return of the trusted goods. Therefore, this fiduciary title gives enough power to retain the possession of the goods being the object of *fiducia* until the debt is paid in total (*ius retentionis*).

274. But the main application of the fiduciary's *ius retentionis* takes effect for the period of time during which the debt is still not payable on demand ('security period'). If the debtor-settlor does not pay it when the debt becomes payable, the creditor-fiduciary will not be interested in retaining the possession of the trusted goods but in putting the guarantee into effect in accordance with the terms named.

In this sense, it is problematical that the contracting parties have agreed that, in the event of non-fulfilment of the debt, the creditor-fiduciary may permanently and automatically appropriate the goods that constitute the object of the *fiducia*. Such an agreement would conflict with the prohibition of *pactum de lex comisoria*, which is clearly laid down in Spanish CC in relation to guarantee real rights, such as pledge and mortgage.[170] By virtue of this *pactum*, the creditor, should the debtor not pay the guaranteed debt, is allowed to appropriate the trusted goods directly and is

169. The debtor is said to have a right to redemption in relation to the goods fiduciarily transferred. *See* S. Cámara Lapuente, *Operaciones fiduciarias o trusts en Derecho español, Revista Crítica de Derecho Inmobiliario*, 1794 (September–October 1999).

170. On guarantee real rights, *see infra* Part V.

not required to proceed to a mandatory sale of it. The majority of scholars,[171] generalizing the solution for pledge and mortgage,[172] believe that the *pactum de lex comisoria* must be considered forbidden for all the guarantee contracts that imply the delivery of debtor's goods into the hands of the creditor.

Nevertheless, the prohibition at issue intends to avoid the creditor becoming unfairly rich at the debtor's expense, which could happen if the creditor were endowed with the power to appropriate debtor's goods whose value is disproportionally higher than the credit's amount directly. Therefore, there are scholars who believe it is possible to agree to such a *pactum* within a fiduciary contract *cum creditore*, provided that (a) the *pactum* is agreed with an express character; (b) the value of the goods, the object of the *fiducia*, does not surpass the credit's amount; and (c) an objective method of appraisal of the goods has been foreseen.[173] However, if there is a disproportion between the value of the trusted goods and the credit's amount, the prohibition of the *pactum de lex comisoria* must prevail.[174]

275. A second system that debtor-settlor and creditor-fiduciary may agree to in order to put the guarantee into effect would consist of permitting, after the debt is unfulfilled, the creditor to demand the mandatory sale of the goods, through either a judicial process or a notarial one, in such a manner that the money obtained in the auction is first assigned to the payment of the credit, and only if there is a remainder will this be given to the debtor-settlor (*ius distrahendi*). This mechanism, which must be considered perfectly valid, is the same that the CC states in order to put the guarantee into effect when the creditor has a right of pledge or mortgage upon one of the debtor's goods (Article 1858 CC).[175]

276. Apart from the acts suitable for the aim of guarantee, the fiduciary does not have the power to alienate the trusted goods in favour of third parties. Nevertheless, if, by breaking the *pactum fiduciae*, the fiduciary has transferred the trusted goods onerously to a third party in good faith, the debtor-settlor will not be able to retrieve the goods, although he/she will always have the opportunity to demand to be compensated for damages.

171. Also the jurisprudence: *See* SSTS 26 Apr. 2001 (*RJA* 2001, 2037), 30 May 2008 (*RJA* 2008, 3190).
172. According to Art. 1859 CC, 'the creditor may not appropriate the goods given under pledge or mortgage, nor alienate them'.
173. *See* S. Cámara Lapuente, *Operaciones fiduciarias o trusts en Derecho español, Revista Crítica de Derecho Inmobiliario*, 1805 (September–October 1999).
174. One more reason for the prohibition of the *pactum de lex comisoria* is connected with the fact that it can cause an alteration on the basis of the principle *par condicio creditorum* because it implies giving a privilege to one of the debtor's creditors to the detriment of the others. *See* R. Durán Rivacoba, *La propiedad en garantía. Prohibición del pacto comisorio* 96 (Aranzadi 1998).
175. On the process to put the guarantee real rights such as pledge or mortgage into effect, *see infra* Part V.

§2. SALE WITH CLAUSE OF SELLING BACK TO THE VENDOR

277. The sale with clause of selling back to the vendor, which is foreseen in Articles 1507 et seq. of Spanish CC, causes an effect very similar to that of the fiduciary conveyance *cum creditore*. In this kind of sale, the vendor keeps in his/her hands the right to retrieve the object sold under certain circumstances.

Although the clause of selling back is shaped as a vendor's right, Article 1507 CC makes this right depending not only – which is obvious – on the return of the price paid to the vendee, together with a series of expenses, but also on the fulfilment of 'anything else that the contracting parties had agreed'.

278. It is true that the sale with clause of selling back to the vendor can serve as an aim other than guaranteeing the payment of a debt that the vendor must assume before the vendee. The vendor could be interested in retrieving the object sold *a posteriori*, and the vendee could be interested in enjoying the thing sold for a period of time (between the time of the sale and the time when the vendor exercises the right to retrieve the object sold), provided that it is guaranteed that he/she will be able to recover the price paid, together with the expenses caused by the contract, as well as the sums invested in order to preserve the object and to make improvements (Article 1518 CC).

Nevertheless, one is confronted with a modality of sale that adapts itself well to the outline of the *fiducia cum creditore*, for example, when the contracting parties agreed that the sum that the vendor owes to the vendee is compensated with the sale's price. The vendor admits that the price has been paid, and the vendee receives the title upon the object sold, but this is not a definitive title because the vendor may exercise the right to retrieve the object sold when he/she has 'returned' the sale's price (i.e., the amount of the debt that the vendor had previously contracted before the vendee) to the vendee.

As it can easily be observed, the delivery of the object sold to the vendee fulfils a function of guarantee with regard to the 'return' of the price (i.e., payment of the debt) because neither the vendor is interested in selling nor is the vendee interested in buying. The TS has given its approval to the validity of a sale with a clause of selling back to the vendor agreed with an aim of guarantee, and it has said that this kind of sale can be qualified as a case of *fiducia cum creditore*. However, the TS has forbidden that the contracting parties agree that the fiduciary-creditor (i.e., the vendee) may directly take the object sold in case of non-fulfilment of the guaranteed debt.[176] Furthermore, it must be taken into account that the *fiducia* agreement is not effective in front of third parties in good faith because it has only an *inter partes* efficacy.[177]

279. The fiduciary character of the vendee's title is shown by the solid position of the vendor before the hypothetical third parties who acquire the object sold from the vendee's hands. According to Article 1510 CC, the vendor is entitled to retrieve

176. *See* SSTS 26 Apr. 2001 (*RJA* 2001, 2037), 30 May 2008 (*RJA* 2008, 3190).

177. *See* SSTS 17 Jul. 2001 (*RJA* 2001, 6860), 5 Dec. 2001 (*RJA* 2001, 9934), 17 Sep. 2003 (*RJA* 2003, 6419).

the object sold in front of any possessor whose right comes from the vendee, even if in the second contract the existence of the clause of selling back has not been mentioned. Nevertheless, Article 1510 CC makes an exception to what the LH states, which means that, in the field of immovable goods, every clause of selling back that is not recorded will not be opposable to third parties who have acquired the goods onerously and in good faith.

Part V. Security

Introduction

280. In this part of the monograph all the mechanisms that, with *erga omnes* efficacy, are used to secure or guarantee a right of credit will be studied.

With general character, the basic premise is that the debtor is responsible for the fulfilment of his/her obligations with his/her patrimony as a whole, both present and future. This is the so-called principle of debtor's universal patrimonial liability, which is reflected in Article 1911 CC. Therefore, when the debtor does not pay a debt due and payable on demand, the creditor may act judicially against the debtor requesting the seizure of enough goods of his/her patrimony.

Depending on the nature of the goods, it may be necessary to convert them into money. This is the case of goods such as buildings, jewellery, or works of art that need to be sold through public auction first to deliver the price to the creditor for the satisfaction of his/her credit subsequently. However, cash money, bank accounts, and exchangeable currency will be delivered directly to the creditor.[178]

When there are several creditors that claim against the debtor for the payment of his/her credits, and the debtor's patrimony is not enough to satisfy all the credits, the general rule is that every creditor has the right to be paid under the same conditions as the rest of them (*par condicio creditorum*), in such a manner that every credit will be satisfied pro rata parte.[179]

281. But, beyond this general scheme, the creditor may get a higher level of safety, characterized by (a) the certainty that his/her credit will be paid even though the debtor's patrimony is not enough to satisfy the debt; or (b) the certainty that his/her credit will be paid before others, in case the debtor's patrimony is not enough to pay all the debts he/she owes:

(a) First, the creditor may agree with the debtor regarding the constitution of a security, that is, a guarantee real right. Securities are a powerful intensifier of creditor's position because in the case of the debtor's non-fulfilment, they give the former the right to request the mandatory sale of the goods in which the security lies, as well as to apply the price so obtained to the satisfaction of his/her credit. Securities alter the functioning of the principle of debtor's universal patrimonial liability because they imply a tie of guarantee between specific goods

178. On the judicial seizure procedure, *see* Arts 584 et seq. LEC.
179. This is a rule subject to a certain number of exceptions, as can be seen *infra*.

in the debtor's patrimony and a definite credit in such a manner that this link is maintained even though the debtor alienates the goods to a third party.[180] In other words, securities have *erga omnes* efficacy because the creditor keeps a *ius destrahendi* although the goods are not yet in the debtor's patrimony. In addition, securities may have been *ab initio* purchased in goods belonging to a third party's patrimony, of course, with his/her consent, regardless of why the third party is ready to give patrimonial support to the debtor.

(b) Besides the possibility of purchasing securities in concrete goods, belonging either to the debtor or to a third party, the law states that some creditors enjoy a preference to be paid before others. The creditor whose credit is preferential knows that, in case of the debtor's insolvency, his/her credit will be satisfied before others. Usually, the term 'privilege' is used to refer to the preference for payment that some creditors enjoy before others (the so-called privileged credits). Obviously, the existence of privileged creditors implies an exception to the principle of *par condicio creditorum*. Because the remaining creditors are affected inevitably by them, preferential credits have a doubtless opposability before third parties (*erga omnes* efficacy). Unlike securities, preferences presuppose the concurrence of several creditors, all of them with the purpose of requesting payment from the same debtor, whose patrimony however is not enough to satisfy all of them. Although some preferences fall upon determined goods in the debtor's patrimony, they do not imply per se the power to impose a distraint on the goods, especially if they have passed into the hands of a third party. However, as we will see below, some privileges given by the law to certain creditors are based on the fact that their credits are secured credits.

282. There are some other mechanisms that, not being securities *stricto sensu*, or regardless of the preferential character of the credit, give the creditor a higher level of safety. This happens with the so-called retention right because some creditors, because of their credit – they have some debtor's goods under their control (e.g., the person in charge of doing some works in a debtor's movables) – may retain in possession the debtor's goods until the debtor satisfies them the corresponding debt. In this part, the 'direct action' will also be examined, which allows the creditor to oppose his/her right before a third party – debtor of the former's debtor.

Finally, the set-off of the credit that the creditor holds against the debtor, with other credit that at the same time the debtor has against the former, may also fulfil a guarantee function. This compensation gives the creditor the possibility of satisfying his/her credit applying the value of an element in the debtor's patrimony, as it is the credit that the debtor himself/herself has against the former creditor. The detraction of this active, in case of creditors' concurrence, means a decrease in the patrimonial basis for guaranteeing the rest of the creditors' claims, and it therefore means a sort of preference for the payment in favour of the setting-off creditor.

---

180. Apart from that, however, the principle of debtor's universal patrimonial liability remains unchanged, which means that the creditor may also impose a distraint on other goods in the debtor's patrimony.

283. Other formulas of guarantee that have only *inter partes* efficacy will remain out of this field of study. They are known under Spanish Law as the so-called personal securities, but these securities, which give the creditor the power to direct in an alternative or subsidiary way against the patrimony of a person different from the debtor, are based on the contractual relation between the creditor and this person (depositor, guarantor). Likewise, the generic measures to protect the credit, such as the creditor's action to cancel exceptionally a contract signed by his/her debtor together with other contracting party, or the action that lets the creditor subrogate the debtor in a definite contractual position in front of a third party, will not be studied.[181] Because these actions are available for every kind of creditors, they do not give a larger than normal dose of security.

181. *See* Arts 1111 and 1291.3 CC.

Chapter 1. Securities in Immovable Property (*See Also* Parts I and IV)

§1. Privileges, Liens and Charges

I. Introduction

284. Besides mortgage, which is doubtless the paradigm of immovable real guarantees, there are other categories that, just as mortgage, fall upon a concrete immovable in a debtor's patrimony and fulfil a function of either guaranteeing the payment of a debt or giving a preference for the satisfaction of the claim.

Under this epigraph, one will first examine the privileges with which some credits are endowed in relation to definite debtor's immovable goods. Second, some guarantee mechanisms such as the retention of title-clause or the rescission-clause will be studied, which are very frequent in the context of the sales on credit of immovable goods. They both guarantee the seller the payment of the whole deferred price. Third, a case of immovable burden, by virtue of which the immovable good is compulsorily affected to the fulfilment of a duty, will be analysed.

II. Immovable Privileges

285. The CC contains a classification of credits, intended for their graduation and payment in case a certain number of creditors have a common insolvent debtor. The classification distinguishes (a) credits that enjoy preference in relation to specific movable goods in a debtor's patrimony (Article 1922 CC); (b) credits that enjoy preference related to debtor's immovable goods (Article 1923 CC); and (c) other privileged credits (Article 1924 CC).[182] Furthermore, the CC provides rules to grade the various types of privileged credits belonging to all of these three categories (*see*, respectively, Articles 1926, 1927, and 1929 CC).

Nevertheless, a new classification of credits, based on other criteria of preference and priority, has been inserted in Law 22/2003 (9 July 2003), on Insolvency (*see* Articles 89–93). When this Law came into force in September 2004, the rules on classification of credits in the CC applied only to non-collective execution proceedings against the debtor. This Law was modified in 2009 (Royal decree Law 3/2009) in order to promote the re-funding of the companies as an alternative to bankruptcy and to make easier these collective execution proceedings.

286. Credits that enjoy a preference in relation to a debtor's definite immovable goods exclude all others to the extent of their amount until the valuation of the immovable at issue. According to Article 1923 CC, these claims are as follows:

182. The expression *special privileges* is used to refer to the ones that fall upon definite goods, movable or immovable, of the debtor, and the term *general privileges* is used for referring to other credits that, although endowed with a preference for the payment, do not fall upon any definite goods in the debtor's patrimony.

(1) credits against the taxpayer in favour of the State (that is, in favour of any public administration) for the amount of the last annuity, matured and unpaid, of the taxes existing on the immovable;[183]
(2) credits in favour of insurance companies corresponding to the premiums of the last two annuities, related to the value of the insured immovable;
(3) mortgage credits and credits coming from the rebuilding or reparation of the goods, provided that they are both registered in the Land Registry, with regard to the mortgaged goods or the rebuilt/repaired goods, respectively;
(4) credits that are provisionally recorded in the Land Registry, because of a seizure, regarding the value of the seized goods; and
(5) finally, the credits coming from the rebuilding or reparation of the immovable although they have not been registered are also privileged. However, this privilege is opposable only before credits other than the ones mentioned in the four paragraphs above.

287. In the case in which two or more privileged credits lie in the debtor's same immovable goods, the following hierarchical criteria must be taken into account:

(1) The credits mentioned in paragraphs 1 and 2 of Article 1923 CC will be paid firstly, in its proper order, according to what has been transcribed *supra*.
(2) The credits mentioned in paragraphs 3 and 4 of Article 1923 CC will be satisfied in the order corresponding to the date of their respective entries in the Land Registry.
(3) Finally, the credits mentioned in paragraph 5 of Article 1923 CC will benefit from preference among themselves according to their seniority.[184]

288. If there is an amount remaining after paying the privileged credits related to a debtor's certain immovable goods, this amount should be added to the debtor's other goods for payment of the rest of the debts.

If, on the contrary, some of the credits with a special immovable privilege have been not completely satisfied, they should be treated, according to their nature, as general privileged credits provided that they can be included in any of the cases described in Article 1924 CC, or as common credits without any kind of privilege in the opposite case.

As regards the collective execution proceedings, Articles 89–93 Law 22/2003 (July 2003) must be examined. This Law is intended to reduce the number of privileged credits (in relation with the ones foreseen in the CC). For instance, those coming from the recording of a seizure in the Land Registry must be considered as ordinary credits – non-privileged – in a collective execution proceeding.

183. Such a privilege is confirmed by the laws on taxes.
184. This rule comes from the fact that the recent expenses made for the rebuilding or reparation of an estate are doubtless the ones that have given place to the less amortized improvements.

III. Securities in the Sale on Credit of Immovable Goods

289. The buyer's duty to pay the deferred price in a sale contract of immovable goods admits to be secured through two different means, both of them liable to produce effects against third parties (buyer's creditors or potential sub-purchasers of the property or other real right in the goods sold). First, one will examine a mechanism frequently used in this type of contracts, as it is the clause that foresees the automatic cancellation of the contract on vendor's demand for the lack of payment of the deferred price. Second, the role of the retention of title-clause in the field of the purchase contracts related to immovable goods is worth mentioning.

290. In the sale of immovable goods with deferred price, the parties may agree that the lack of payment will give the vendor the power to rescind the contract (Article 1504 CC). As it is known, the main consequence of the rescission is that the parties return to the positions that they would have occupied if the contract had not been made. Accordingly, they both remain released from further obligations to each other, but at the same time, they must mutually return whatever they had received under the contract.

Thanks to a rescission-clause expressly inserted in the contract, the vendor obtains the guarantee that the immovable object of the sale will return to his patrimony in case of non-fulfilment of the vendee's duty related to the payment of the deferred price. In this way, it is secured that, although the buyer does not satisfy the part of the price not still paid, the vendor will not suffer any damage to his/her property.

291. Nevertheless, the effect of such a rescission-clause is not automatic. When the obligation of payment of the deferred price is not fulfilled, the vendor has the power to demand the rescission through either a judicial or a notarial request. Before this request is formally made, and although the deadline has already expired, the buyer may still pay and be released from his/her contractual obligations. Due to this fact, it is said that this kind of rescission-clauses has voluntary effects for the seller, who may choose to bring an action against the buyer to obtain the (delayed) fulfilment of the contract.

After the vendor has exercised the right to which the rescission-clause entitles him/her, the effects will apply retroactively to the time when the non-fulfilment occurred (which may be relevant, for example, to obligate the vendee to return fruits or rents received from the goods sold). Moreover, the vendor's decision is irreversible: Neither the buyer may pay with releasing effects nor may the seller request the payment of the price through an action aimed at the fulfilment of the contract.

292. The clause one is talking about may be recorded in the Land Registry. When such a registration has been made, it will be opposable to third parties whose right derives from the vendee. Indeed, according to Article 11 LH, this is one of the only two ways to achieve the opposability beyond the parties of the price's deferment in the purchase of immovable goods.[185] Thus, when the rescission-clause has been registered, the vendor's request of rescission will affect not only the buyer but also any sub-purchaser of the goods at issue.

293. As regards the retention of title-clause, it is above all used in the sale on credit of movable goods,[186] although it is inserted with certain frequency into contracts of sale on credit of immovable goods. By means of this clause, the parties agree that the transfer of the property of the goods sold will be deferred until the buyer completely pays the price. It implies an exception to the general principle according to which the transfer of the property is linked to the delivery of the object sold into the buyer's hands.

After the conclusion of the contract and before the total payment of the price, the vendee does not purchase the property in them, although the vendor has made the delivery of the goods. Therefore, the buyer may not alienate them, although he/she is allowed to use and enjoy them, taking care to keep their integrity. Contrarily, the vendor may not alienate the goods sold because the buyer's purchase depends only on the total payment of the price. After this payment is made, the property will pass to the buyer *ipso iure*.

294. The retention of title-clause is liable to be registered in the Land Registry (Articles 9.2 and 23 LH). Lack of registration means that the seller will not be able to oppose his/her right in front of subsequent purchasers who, with onerous title and in good faith, have purchased the goods from the vendee (Article 34 LH). Thus, the seller will always be able to assert his/her right before subsequent purchasers that either knew of the existence of the retention of title-clause or were endowed with a gratuitous title. Although the seller may not claim the goods in the possession of a third party, he/she will be able however to bring an action against the vendee.

However, the retention of title-clause is opposable before the buyer's creditors, in such a manner that the vendor may stop any seizure at the request of these creditors upon the goods sold.[187]

IV. The Real Burden in the Joint Ownership of Blocks of Flats

295. The joint ownership of blocks of flats is subject to special statutory provisions, as has already been studied.[188] The owners of the various flats or premises are vested in a mixed right: on the one hand, the exclusive ownership of his/her flat

185. The other one would consist in guaranteeing the payment of the deferred price by means of mortgage, as Art. 11 LH also points out.
186. As we will observe *infra* Ch. 2, §1. *See also supra* Part II, para. 215.
187. Because the property belongs to him/her and not to the buyer. The action granted to the vendor and proprietor in such a case has been called 'action derived from a third party's property'. It is an action brought by the actual owner of goods unduly seized against both the person who suffers the seizure and the person who started the seizure proceedings. On this action, *see supra* Part I, para. 93.
188. *See supra* Part I, Ch. 6, §1, II. A.

or premises; and on the other hand, the co-ownership in the common elements of the building. The addition of these two elements defines the participation quota of every owner in the total property in the building.

Every owner has, among other duties, the duty to contribute to the general expenses of the building not liable to individualization, in proportion to his/her quota, from which a right of credit in favour of the members of the joint ownership as a whole arises.

296. According to Article 9.1.e) LPH, the new owner who purchases a flat or premises in a block of flats submitted to the special joint ownership that the LPH describes assumes the responsibility for paying the fees overdue owed by the previous holder to the joint ownership because of his/her contribution to the general expenses of the building. The flat or premises at issue will be subject to the fulfilment of this duty under two conditions: (1) the new owner assumes this responsibility within the limit given by the value of the flat or premises; and (2) the responsibility assumed by the new owner reaches only to fees overdue corresponding to the annuity in course and the three previous ones.

§2. Mortgage

I. Concept and General Features

297. Mortgage is a guarantee real right that falls, in its standard modality, upon immovable goods.[189] As a guarantee right, it is used to secure the fulfilment of a duty; and as a real right, it empowers its holder to request the mandatory sale of the goods to apply the price so obtained for the satisfaction of his/her right, in case of non-fulfilment of the guaranteed obligation.

Rules on mortgage are contained in Articles 1857–1862 and 1874 et seq. CC, as well as in Articles 104 et seq. LH. Besides these general rules, other special mortgage-laws must be mentioned. In a chronological order, one is talking about the Law on Regulation of the Mortgage Market (1981), the Law on Subrogation and Modification of Mortgage Loans (1994), the Law 41/2007 – which modifies some dispositions of the two latter, introducing as well the so-called reverse mortgage – the Law 2/2009 (31 March) on Mortgage contracts between consumers and finance companies that are not banks, and the more recent Law 1/2013, of 14 May, on measures to reinforce the protection to loan mortgage debtors.

298. The mortgage is really a real right, in such a way that the mortgagee has not only a preference for the satisfaction of his/her credit in front of other creditors,[190] but he/she may also pursue the mortgaged estate and request the forced sale of it regardless of the current person to whom the mortgaged estate belongs.

---

189. There is also the possibility of constituting a mortgage upon movable goods, as will be seen in detail *infra* Ch. 2.
190. He/she enjoys this preference in the terms that have been said *supra* §1, II.

The mortgage is a limited real right or a right in another person's goods. The owner of a mortgaged estate continues to maintain his/her ownership, and especially the powers to use and enjoy the estate, given that the mortgage does not imply transfer of possession in favour of the mortgagee. The owner of the mortgaged estate even keeps the power to sell the estate or to constitute limited real rights in it. But, of course, the estate will be transferred with the burden that the mortgage means, in such a way that the purchaser may not avoid that, in case of non-fulfilment of the guaranteed debt, the estate is mandatorily sold at the request of the mortgagee.

The main feature of the right of mortgage is mortgagee's power to demand the forced sale of the estate at public auction (*ius distrahendi*). After the estate has been sold, the price so obtained will be applied to satisfy the mortgagee's claim.

The mortgage is an accessory right to the obligation that it guarantees. It is the existence of this obligation that justifies the mortgage's existence. Thus, the extinction of the secured credit (e.g., because it has been paid completely) implies the extinction of the mortgage. Nevertheless, because of the accessory character of the mortgage, the holder of the secured credit must always be the holder of the mortgage, which means that the mortgage may not be conveyed separately from the guaranteed credit.

Finally, it is worthwhile to underscore the fact that the mortgage needs to be registered in the Land Registry, not only in order to obtain its *erga omnes* efficacy but also to achieve a mere *inter partes* efficacy. This exceptional feature must be related to the fact that the mortgage does not comprehend the transfer of possession to the mortgagee. Furthermore, the purchase of a mortgage needs to be stated in a notarial deed because private documents may not be recorded in the Land Registry (*see* Articles 1875 CC and 145.1 LH).

II. Subjects and Object

299. In every mortgage relationship there are at least two people: on the one side, the holder of both the mortgage and the secured credit (mortgagee); and on the other side, the owner of the mortgaged estate, who normally is at the same time the debtor of the guaranteed debt (mortgager), although he/she could be a third party that accepts the fact that one of his/her goods is mortgaged to guarantee another's obligation. Indeed, after the mortgage exists the debtor may also transfer the mortgaged estate to a third party, which means that the roles of mortgager and owner of the mortgaged estate must not necessarily be fulfilled by the same person.

Special legal requirements of pre-contractual information and contractual formalities for the mortgage loan (among other rules) are mandatory in the case in which the debtor is a consumer (a person who acts without a professional aim). These requirements have been established by the Law 2/2009 (31 March) on Mortgage contracts with consumers. The new legal measures are supposed to bring the consumer a higher protection when he/she is asking for a mortgage loan that will fall – the real guarantee – upon an object of his/her ownership.

His/her position of inferiority before the other contractual party (usually, a bank) had moved the Spanish Administration to put the Banks' mortgage loan contracting under control and supervision of the Central Bank of Spain. All this has taken place in 1994 (when some rules about the matter were published), but a new goal is trying to be achieved recently: supervising finance companies other than banks that offer mortgage loans to consumers without being under any control of the Central Bank of Spain (because of the fact that they are not banks *stricto sensu*).

In order to do that, the Law 2/2009 has created a public Register in which all these companies must be recorded before the beginning of their activities, as well as the obligation for them to guarantee the economical damages they could cause by contracting a civil liability insurance or a bank collateral.

Referring to loan agreements with consumers we have also to take into account Directive 1993 on unfair terms in consumer contracts. Several terms introduced by Spanish Banks in their mortgage loans contracts with consumers have been declared unfair by the TS. For instance, in variable-rate loan agreements[191] the one that establishes a *minimum* below which the interest rate cannot descend for the benefit of the Bank, for example 1.5% (the so-called ground clause). But, on the other hand, this *minimum* is not accompanied by the fixation of a *maximum* for the benefit of the debtor (consumer). Or, if so, the *maximum* is so high that is way too difficult for the consumer to take advantage of it, for example 10% (the so-called cap clause). The TS has stated that Banks have the obligation to give the debtors enough information about the meaning and the reach of this clause. This clause must be clearly separated from the rest of the contractual terms and highlighted in order to let the consumer know not only its existence but the economic risks of its application. Otherwise it will be considered unfair and, as a consequence of it, declared invalid (SSTS 10 May 2013, 13 October 2014, 15 February 2015, 24 March 2015). So, according to these rulings, floor clauses, in themselves, were not illegal. These clauses were deemed illegal when they were applied unfairly and when the financial institution did not properly inform the consumer of their presence in the contract. Banks were, therefore, obliged to explain the terms of the mortgage contract in a comprehensive way to all kinds of consumers. If these conditions were not met the clause will be considered null and void.

Nevertheless, the TS dismissed the petition by which plaintiffs were seeking an order of sued banks to pay back to their clients the amounts unduly collected by application of the floor clauses. In a contested provision, the TS resolved that the declaration of nullity of the floor clauses did not have any retroactive effects, so banks were not obliged to pay back the amounts unduly collected, founding such decision in the necessity to preserve legal certainty and to avoid consequences against country's economic stability and general interests.

Since then, lawsuits filed by individuals and households demanding the nullity of the floor clauses along with an order to the sued banks to pay back the amounts unduly collected are being ruled by the First Instance Courts. The rulings so far have mainly accepted the claims in full, condemning banks to pay back the amounts. So we are in fact assisting in a sort of revolution as the lower Courts do not apply the criteria set out in the mentioned TS ruling.

191. In Spain mortgage variable-rate loan agreements are usually submitted to the Euribor ("Euro Interbank Offered Rate"). The Euribor rates are based on the average interest rates at which a large panel of European banks borrows funds from the another.

Most of the rulings of the first instance courts are based on the general provision set out in Article 1303 of the CC, whose application was avoided by the TS of the grounds of the preservation of general interest. According to this rule, the nullity of a contractual provision implies the obligation of the parties to give back or to undo all what they have received by virtue of the null provision.

One of these first instance courts (Juzgado de lo Mercantil de Granada) decided to refer to the Court of Justice some questions for a preliminary ruling. To be more specific, it has asked the Court of Justice if the non retroactivity rule is compatible with the aims of Directive 1993 on unfair terms in consumer contracts.

The European Court of Justice (ECJ) Judgment of 21 December 2016 (Case C-154/15) held that Article 6(1) of Directive 1993 must be interpreted as precluding national case-law that temporally limits the restitutory effects connected with a finding of unfairness by a court, in accordance with Article 3(1) of that Directive, in respect of a clause contained in a contract concluded between a consumer and a seller or supplier, to amounts overpaid under such a clause after the delivery of the decision in which the finding of unfairness is made.

As a consequence, the Spanish TS Judgement of 24 February 2017[192] changed its prior doctrine and ruled in favour the restitution of the amounts overpaid in application of the unfair clause.

Last but not least, a new type of mortgage – with special subjective requirements – has been introduced in Spain recently. One concerns the ‘reverse mortgage’, regulated by Law 41/2007 (7 December).

From the point of view of the subject who is asking for a mortgage loan, the ‘reverse mortgage’ (or lifetime mortgage) is provided to bring economical support to those people who are more than 65 years old (or handicapped) and own the house in which they live. The mechanism of this real guarantee is the following: The senior (or the handicapped) receives an amount of money (credit) from the loaner by means of the payment of periodical rents until his/her death (or until a certain deadline stated in the contract). His/her home is attached to this guarantee (mortgaged object). That amount of money, and all the interests produced during this time, must be returned to the loaner when the debtor dies. When that takes place, the debtor’s inheritors have two different alternatives: either paying the debt by selling (or not) the mortgaged estate or accepting the foreclosure of the house. The Law foresees several measures in order to reduce the costs of that credit, especially related to the exemption of the taxes that are applicable in those cases.

300. As regards the term *object* (of the mortgage), two different senses are used. First, it refers to the right (not necessarily property) on which the mortgage falls. Second, it is used to mean the accessory elements in an estate that are burdened by the mortgage together with the estate itself.

301. The right of property is the primary right of all the rights liable to be mortgaged. However, apart from property, other limited real rights of an immovable

192. *RJA* 2017/602.

nature are liable to be mortgaged. Depending on the content of the mortgaged right, the guarantee will have a larger or smaller extent.[193]

302. In relation to the mortgage's extent, it must be clarified whether some accessory elements such as accessions, improvements, fruits, easements, movable goods set within the estate, or compensations paid to the owner resulting from an accident or an expropriation should be considered as mortgaged together with the estate.

303. According to Article 534 CC and Articles 109, 110 LH, 111.1 *a contrario* LH, the following are considered as mortgaged together with the mortgaged estate, although not mentioned in the contract: (a) natural accessions; (b) industrial accessions, that is, improvement works, although only the ones consisting of new plantings or works for irrigation, drainage, reparation, safety, transformation, comfort, decoration, or elevation of the already existing buildings. The improvements that suppose either artificial aggregations of terrains or constructions of a building *ex novo* are expressly excluded;[194] (c) compensations assigned or due to the owner because of the mortgaged goods, resulting from accidents occurring after the purchase of the mortgage or because of the expropriation for public utility of the mortgaged estate; (d) movable goods that are within the estate in such a way that they cannot be separated without being damaged or without damaging the estate itself; and (e) easements in which regard the mortgaged estate is the dominant estate.

304. On the contrary, there are certain elements not burdened by the mortgage unless agreed to otherwise by the parties (*see* Article 111 LH): (a) movable goods situated on the estate in a permanent way for its decoration, comfort, service or exploitation that may be separated without damage to them or to the estate itself; (b) fruits produced by the estate, regardless of whether they are pending production, are pending harvesting, or have been harvested; (c) rents produced by the estate, matured but still not paid at the time the fulfilment of the guaranteed obligation is requested.

305. The objective extent of the mortgage bears important modulations when the mortgaged estate has been acquired by a third party (the so-called, 'third possessor' (of the mortgaged estate)).[195] Article 112 LH indicates, with imperative character,[196] that in this case, the mortgage will be extended neither to the movable goods situated permanently on the estate by the third possessor, nor to the improvements paid by him/her (with some exceptions), nor to the pending fruits or overdue rents belonging to the third possessor.

---

193. *See* Art. 107 LH, which mentions several rights such as usufruct, bare ownership, easements, building and planting rights, goods already mortgaged, and the right of the vendor in the sale with clause of selling back.

194. Which, however, may be included in the mortgage by express agreement of the parties.

195. The word '*possessor*' in the expression *third possessor of mortgaged estate* is not used in a strict technical-juridical sense. The correct expression would be *third purchaser* or *third owner* of the mortgaged estate, but the successful expression has been the first one.

196. That is, beyond what is agreed to by the parties in the mortgage contract.

III. Extent of the Mortgage Related to the Guaranteed Obligation

306. The mortgage may be constituted to guarantee any kind of obligations (Article 105 LH), but the guaranteed obligation normally has pecuniary character, in such a way that it consists of an amount of money or at least is convertible into money. The rules on Land Registry foresee that in every record of a right of mortgage in the Registry the amount of money into which the guaranteed obligation can be converted (Article 12 LH) must be stated or, in its place, the maximum amount that the mortgaged estate secures.

307. Because the guaranteed debt has, directly or indirectly, pecuniary nature, it is necessary to clarify whether the interest eventually produced by the debt – understood as a capital – is secured by the mortgage as well. In order to solve this question, a distinction between remunerative and moratory interest is needed. Remunerative interest is the one that serves to pay for the enjoyment of someone else's sum of money for a certain term. It is very common that parties in a loan contract agree to the payment of remunerative interest.

Contrarily, moratory interest is simply aimed to punish the debtor because of a delay in the fulfilment of his/her obligation. Article 1108 CC, assuming that money has an inherent ability for producing interest, provides that the delay in the payment of an amount of money gives the creditor the right to obtain interest as a way of compensating him/her for damages incurred. This moratory interest will adjust to the rate agreed upon by the parties or, for lack of contractual provision, to the money's legal rate.[197]

308. As regards remunerative interest, the mortgage guarantees in principle the total amount it reaches (Article 146 LH). Indeed, this amount must be recorded in the mortgage's entry together with the amount corresponding to the capital of the debt.[198] Accordingly, regardless of the time when the capital must be paid, the mortgagee may bring proceedings against the mortgager for the remunerative interest due and not paid. However, there is a protection rule in favour of the third purchaser of the mortgaged estate, in relation to the extent the remunerative interest is secured by the mortgage, which limits the guarantee to the interest produced for the two last years and the current annuity (Article 114 LH).

309. Moratory interest, however, is secured only by the mortgage when expressly stated in the contract by the parties concerned. Given its uncertain nature, it is necessary that the mortgage's entry in the Land Registry indicates the maximum amount of responsibility that the mortgaged estate secures in relation to the moratory interest.

---

197. The legal rate of interest of money is fixed for each annuity by the Law of State General Budget. For the period corresponding to 2016, it was set at a rate of 3%. Law 1/2013, of 14 May, on measures to reinforce the protection to loan mortgage debtors has set a limit for this kind of interest in loan agreements secured by a mortgage upon the debtor's family home. It cannot be higher than three times the legal interest.
198. The capital of a debt is also called 'principal amount', or even simply 'principal', of that debt.

IV. Content of the Right

310. The mortgage right is composed of two main powers, corresponding to each of the phases that the mortgage may go through. During the first phase, when the guaranteed debt is not yet due, or when the debtor is paying the parts of the debt as they are due (the so-called safety phase), the mortgagee has the power to maintain the value of the mortgaged estate. In a possible second phase (which may be called 'foreclosure phase'), the mortgagee has the power to request the realization of the mortgaged estate, if the debtor does not fulfil or interrupts the payment of the guaranteed debt.

311. During the safety phase, the mortgagee has the power to preserve the value of the mortgaged estate. It is a cautionary power, previous to the eventual realization of the encumbered goods: Its goal is to secure the effectiveness of the foreclosure, if necessary. The reason for assigning the mortgagee this power lies in the fact that mortgage does not involve possessory transfer in favour of the holder, which generates the risk that the mortgager, who is in possession of the goods, may act to decrease their value, with the corresponding reduction for mortgagee's expectations.

Therefore, Article 117 LH allows the mortgagee to bring an action if the mortgaged estate suffers deterioration producing a relevant decrease in value as a result of the mortgager's fault (i.e., he/she effects a long-duration lease upon the estate in exchange for a very low rent). This action can give place to an injunction whereby the mortgager is instructed to do, or to avoid doing, the necessary action in order to remedy the deterioration.

As a derivation from the right to maintain the value of the goods, the mortgagee is allowed to request the increase of the mortgaged object or to consider the debt mature before the time it was supposed to be due in origin.

312. In case the guaranteed debt is not fulfilled, the mortgagee may request to realize the mortgaged estate. In any case, the mortgagee is allowed to take directly the estate by himself/herself. The foreclosure of the mortgage may be effected through a judicial or a notarial auction, the latter only when expressly stated in the contract.

313. Concerning the judicial foreclosure of the mortgage, Articles 681 et seq. LEC are applicable. These rules describe a fast and simple procedure. They underscore two essential data (which must be indicated in the mortgage deed): the price at which the parties estimate the estate, which will be the basis for the judicial auction, as well as a residence to which the requirements and notifications addressed to the debtor will be mailed. The proceedings may be interrupted only on one of the following grounds: (a) a criminal action has been put in course; (b) a third party has brought an action to claim the ownership of the mortgaged estate based on a title prior to the date of mortgage's registration; or (c) the mortgager opposes the foreclosure because of the extinction either of the security or the guaranteed debt. The remaining grounds alleged by the defendant (for instance, the unfairness of the terms of the loan agreement) will be solved in ordinary proceedings, separate from that of the foreclosure The main problem here is that the ordinary (declaratory) proceedings do not suspend the effect of the enforcement. So even if the Judge in the declaratory proceedings considers – for example – that one or more of the mortgage loan agreement terms are unfair, he has no means to stop the public auction of the family home of the defendant. Once this happens, the situation becomes irreversible, and the debtor would only have the right to claim a monetary compensation. A Spanish Judge (Juzgado de lo Mercantil Núm. 3 of Barcelona) expressed doubts concerning the conformity of Spanish Procedure Law with the legal framework established by the Directive of 1993 on unfair terms in consumer contracts. In those circumstances, he decided to stay the proceedings and refer these doubts to the ECJ for a preliminary ruling. The ECJ stated, in its decision of 14 March 2013, that legislation of a Member State which precludes a debtor from making objections based on the unfairness of the contractual terms during the enforcement proceedings and, *at the same time,* does not permit the Court which does have jurisdiction to assess the unfairness of such a term to grant interim relief to guarantee the full effectiveness of its final decision is against the Directive of 1993. As a consequence of this Judgment, the Spanish Parliament has passed the Law 1/2013 of 14 May, on measures to reinforce the protection to loan mortgage debtors. The influence of the ECJ is clear: From now, the unfairness of a term of the loan mortgage agreement can be alleged by the debtor during the enforcement proceedings (Article 695 LEC).

314. Although the notarial foreclosure procedure had been questioned by the TS because of a problem of hierarchy between rules, it has recently received statutory support. It is possible to use it only when the parties have so agreed (Article 129 LH). In this case, the mandatory sale of the mortgaged estate will be made through the notary, according to the procedure foreseen in Articles 234–236 RH.

315. Both procedures lead to the realization of the mortgaged estate at public auction. The price paid by the buyer will be applied first to the satisfaction of the secured credit, and afterwards the eventual remainder may be used only for the payment of other debts, or left to the own mortgager. However, the mandatory sale of the mortgaged estate does not remove the previous burdens and seizures on the estate recorded in the Land Registry, which will subsist.

The remaining price from the auction does not apply to the extinction of these previous burdens, but the winner of the auction purchases the estate with all these encumbrances. Conversely, the cancellation of every encumbrance recorded after the mortgage at issue will be instructed. The holders of the affected credits may, at the most, try to satisfy themselves with the rest of the price paid at auction.

V. Assignment of the Mortgage Credit and Sale of the Mortgaged Estate

316. Both the mortgagee and the mortgager maintain the power to transfer their respective rights. The former may convey the credit secured with the mortgage, and the latter may sell the burdened estate to a third party (the so-called third possessor (of mortgaged estate)). However, in both cases, the law imposes some conditions.

317. Regarding the conveyance of the secured credit, it must be underscored that, given that the credit is not separable from the right of mortgage, the transfer of the former means necessarily the transfer of the latter. Article 149 LH provides two requisites for such a conveyance: (1) it must be contained in a public document and notified to the mortgager; and (2) it must be registered in the Land Registry. The mortgager's notification is essential in order to neutralize the possibility that he/she becomes released by paying the debt to a person that is no longer his/her creditor, while the registration is congruent with the requisites for putting into effect the mortgage itself.

318. The Law of Subrogation and Modification of Mortgage Loans should also be mentioned on this matter, which allows the mortgager to force a subrogation of the mortgage loan or, alternatively, a modification of the conditions of such a mortgage loan.[199] The Law grants the mortgager the power to subrogate the mortgagee/lender by another financial company without the need for the consent of the former. The mortgager has to borrow the money to pay the first loan from the latter financial entity. The Law allows the first lender to accept the modification of some conditions of the mortgage loan in order to avoid the loss of a client.

319. Although the owner of the mortgaged estate may transfer it, the buyer will acquire it with the encumbrance that the mortgage brings with it. The buyer, because of the mere purchase of the mortgaged estate, does not assume the role of debtor in relation to the debt that the mortgage guarantees. Thus, in principle, the buyer is responsible only up to the value of the mortgaged estate.

The guaranteed debt continues to be linked to the person of the debtor who sold the encumbered estate. However, it is possible that the buyer assumes the guaranteed debt together with the property in the mortgaged estate, which will release the vendor (and previous mortgager) from the obligation to pay. Nevertheless, it is not possible to effect this change of mortgager without the consent of the mortgagee, which may be express or tacit (Article 118 LH).

320. When the purchaser of a mortgaged estate does not assume the debt that the mortgage guarantees, there are two options: (1) to retain the part of the price equivalent to the amount of the guaranteed obligation; or (2) to discount from the price the part corresponding to that amount. In either case, the buyer responds only with the value of the mortgaged immovable:

(a) In the case in which the buyer has retained part of the price, he/she is in charge of verifying the payment of the debt to the mortgagee after the debt is due. It must be understood that the seller receives the total price of the sale, but part of this price is retained by the buyer with the commitment of making the payment in favour of the former.
(b) The other option is that the buyer discounts the part corresponding to the guaranteed debt from the price of the sale. The vendor maintains his/her role not

199. This Law has been modified by Law 41/2007 in relation to the commissions that the banks are allowed to ask in the case of subrogation.

only as mortgager but also as the person in charge of making the payment to the mortgagee. After the obligation is fulfilled, the vendor subrogates the mortgagee until the buyer pays the part of the price that had been discounted.

Chapter 2. Securities in Movable Property

321. In this chapter, several institutions used to guarantee the payment of a debt, or to give the creditor a preference for the payment in front of other creditors but based on the special subjection of debtor's certain movable goods, will be examined (*see also* Parts II and IV). One will see in the first epigraph a description of the privileges that certain creditors enjoy in relation to the value of some movable goods in the debtor's patrimony and the securities normally used in the sale on credit of movable goods. Afterwards, the pledge – the paradigm of movable security – will be studied either in its classical modality (pledge with transfer of possession) or in more modern types (pledge without transfer of possession, movable mortgage).

In the third epigraph, other mechanisms of movable security, not so perfect, will be analysed, such as the retention right and the set-off. Finally, in the fourth epigraph of this chapter, the figure known as 'direct action' will be examined.

§1. Privileges, Liens and Charges

I. Movable Privileges

322. Creditors that enjoy a preference with regard to debtor's definite movable goods exclude all others to the extent of their amount until the valuation of the movable goods at issue (Article 1926 CC).

According to Article 1922 CC, these claims are (a) credits for the price of sale, construction, reparation, or maintenance of goods being in the hands of the debtor; (b) credits secured with pledge; (c) credits secured with a commercial security; (d) credits in favour of the carrier; (e) credits for lodging, in relation to the debtor's movable goods situated in the lodging; (f) credits for seeds and expenses of growing and harvesting, upon the fruits of the harvest in which they were employed; and (g) credits for leases and rents of a year, upon the lessee's movable goods existing in the leased estate and upon the fruits of it (if they correspond to the lessee). In every case it must be understood that the privilege limits itself to the value of the goods that are the object of the right or contract that give place to the former.[200]

323. When two or more privileged credits affect the same movable goods in a debtor's patrimony, the following hierarchical criteria must be taken into account (Article 1926 CC):

(1) The credit secured with pledge excludes every other until the valuation of the goods given as pledge.
(2) In the case in which there are several credits secured with commercial security, the priority parameter will be the date of enforcement of every document.

200. The changes on this matter caused by the coming into force of the new Law on Insolvency must be underscored. *See supra* para. 285.

(3) Credits for seeds and expenses of growing and harvesting will be preferred to the ones coming from leases, with regard to the fruits of the harvest for which the former were used.
(4) Other privileged credits will be satisfied *pro rata parte* until the valuation of the goods.

324. As took place with special immovable privileges, after paying privileged credits, any amount remaining will be added to the debtor's remaining goods for the payment of the non-privileged credits. On the contrary, if one of the specially privileged credits is not completely satisfied, it will be treated either as a general privileged credit – provided that it fits into any of the cases of Article 1924 CC – or as a common credit without any preference.

In the case in which a collective execution proceeding has taken place (because of the debtor's insolvency), one will take into account the special rules coming from the Law 22/2003 (9 July) on Insolvency.

The special movable privileges are foreseen in Article 90, in which you can see, among others, credits guaranteed with legal or voluntary mortgage or pledge without transfer of the possession; credits coming from the production or reparation of movable goods; or credits coming either from the leasing of movables or from the deferred price of its sale.

II. Securities in the Sale on Credit of Movable Goods

325. As in the sale on credit of immovable goods, the obligation of payment of the deferred price in a contract of sale on credit of movable goods may be secured through several mechanisms liable to produce effects before third parties. These mechanisms are described in Law 28/1998 (13 July 1998) on Sale on Credit of Movable Goods, which substituted a previous homonymous one (17 July 1965): the retention of title-clause and to forbid the transfer (the goods sold).

326. Although the retention of title-clause implies that the goods do not pass into the buyer's patrimony until the total payment of the deferred price has been made, to forbid the transfer deprives the buyer of one of every owner's typical powers: the power to alienate the goods that are the object of ownership, despite which the goods sold are in this case within the buyer's patrimony. In both cases, only with the consent of the seller (or the lender) may the buyer transfer the purchased goods in favour of third parties.[201]

327. Obviously, due to the securing of the sale with one of these two mechanisms, the vendor may bring an action against the third parties to whom the goods have been eventually transferred, in case the buyer does not fulfil his/her duty of

201. The lender is mentioned because the law also regulates the contracts in which a subject other than the vendor grants the buyer (or the seller) a loan. In such an event, it is this lender who has to be reimbursed to the extent of the deferred price.

payment. Nevertheless, for these guarantees to be opposable before third parties, they must be registered in the Registry of Movable Goods.[202]

§2. PLEDGE

I. Introduction

328. If mortgage is the paradigmatic guarantee real right in the field of immovable goods, pledge occupies this role in the sphere of movable goods. Thus, the main and first differential element between these two rights is the nature of the object (immovable versus movable) upon which they fall. Second, although the mortgage does not imply the possessory transfer of the mortgaged estate into the mortgagee's hands, the pledge, at least according to the classical regulation in CC and given the movable character of its object, implies the transfer of the possession in favour of the pledge creditor.

However, the conceptual differences between pledge and mortgage have been diluted over the last decades, when certain types of securities, although they burden upon movable goods, are configured as a right of pledge without transfer of possession, or as a right of 'movable mortgage'.

The appearance of these new movable securities that – unlike the classical pledge, which does not imply transfer of possession to the creditor – is linked to the confirmation that depriving the debtor of the possession of the pledged goods can be highly inefficient in some cases, especially when the goods are destined to agrarian or industrial use because then the debtor's economic capacity decreases, and the possibilities for him to fulfil his obligations in a normal way are reduced to the same extent.

Also, the appearance of these new movable securities must be tied to the increasing economic significance – together with the identifiable character – with which many movable goods are currently endowed. This circumstance places them in the category of immovable goods. The existence of new goods (in a legal sense) not easily classifiable as movable or immovable must also be taken into account.

In the following sections, one will initially see the classical regulation of the pledge with transfer of possession, as it is contained in Articles 1857 et seq. CC and particularly in Articles 1863–1873 CC. Subsequently the modern movable securities without transfer of possession will be studied, which are the object of legal treatment in LHMPDP (16 December 1954).

II. Pledge with Possessory Transfer

329. According to its classical description, the pledge could be defined as a guarantee real right that falls upon someone else's movable goods with the goal of securing a debt, and that allows the holder to (a) retain the possession of the object given

202. *See supra* Part II, paras 214–216.

as pledge; and (b) request the mandatory sale of the pledged goods in case of non-fulfilment of the guaranteed debt in order to satisfy the credit with the price so obtained. The creditor whose claim is secured with pledge will be named 'pledge creditor', and the debtor that gives one of his/her movable goods as a pledge for guaranteeing the payment of a debt will be named 'pledge debtor'.

Nevertheless, the person that constitutes the pledge upon goods in his/her patrimony does not necessarily need to be the debtor of the secured obligation, it being possible that a third-party grants a pledge in one of his/her goods to favour – whatever the reason – the debtor (Article 1857 CC).

The pledge does not cause the transfer of property of the pledged goods but only the transfer of possession into the creditor's hands. This possessory conveyance fulfils a function of publicity: Further creditors of the same debtor will be able to know the limits of the latter's solvency because specific goods in his/her patrimony remain burdened in guarantee of a definite credit. In addition, the transfer of possession to the pledge creditor avoids the debtor alienating the pledged goods to third parties in (eventual) good faith, who would deserve protection for trusting in the appearance of ownership that normally arises from the possession.

The pledge creditor may neither alienate the pledged goods while the secured debt is not yet due nor appropriate it directly after the non-fulfilment of the secured obligation (Article 1859 CC). What the pledge creditor does have is the power to request the realization of the pledged goods, for in this manner, by means of the compulsory sale of the goods, he/she is trying to satisfy his/her credit with the price obtained at the auction.

330. Unlike the normal occurrence in the Law of Contracts in Spain, the pledge contract is not a consensual one, but its conclusion requires that the debtor makes the delivery of the pledged goods into the hands of the pledge creditor (Article 1863 CC).

Apart from that, for the pledge to be opposable to third parties, it is necessary that the contract be put in writing by means of a notarial deed (Article 1865 CC).

331. In respect to the power to retain the possession of the goods, the pledge creditor may exercise it by himself/herself or through a third party, designed in the contract by mutual agreement. The retention will last until the payment of the secured obligation, including interest if previously agreed (Articles 1866 and 1871 CC).

The position of the pledge creditor in relation to the power of possessory retention is similar to the contractual position of a depositary because he/she may not use the goods delivered as pledge without consent of the owner (Article 1870 CC). As with the depositary, the pledge creditor must diligently take care of the pledged goods, has the right to be compensated for the expenses made in their maintenance, and is responsible for the goods' loss or damage according to the general rules in the CC (*see* Article 1867 CC). The pledge creditor may, of course, neither alienate the pledged goods nor appropriate them because the pledge debtor continues to be the owner of the pledged goods (Articles 1859 and 1869.I CC). On the contrary, the pledge creditor may exercise actions that correspond to the owner of the pledged goods to reclaim them or to defend them against a third party (Article 1869.II CC).

The pledge creditor may prorogue the possessory retention of the goods given as pledge when the debtor incurs in a second debt with regard to the former, with the understanding that the second debt is due before the first one is paid. The pledge will be automatically extended to this second debt, although only in the aspect of the possessory retention, not in the one of realization of the value of the goods (Article 1866 CC).[203]

332. As regards the power to realize the pledged goods, one already knows that the creditor may request the mandatory sale of these goods after the debtor has not fulfilled the secured obligation. The mandatory sale can be effected through a notarial procedure. If after two consecutive auctions the pledge has not been alienated, the creditor may appropriate the pledged goods, being obliged to give the debtor a document stating that the former recognizes the complete liquidation of the debt. In addition, there is also the possibility of a judicial procedure to make the pledge right effective (*see* Articles 681 et seq. LEC) (Article 1872 CC).

Finally, it cannot be forgotten that the pledge creditor enjoys a preference in relation to the value of the pledged goods (Article 1922.2° CC), and his/her right will receive priority in case of concurrence with holders of other privileged credits in the same goods (Article 1926.1° CC).

III. Movable Securities Without Possessory Transfer

333. The LHMPDP regulates two modalities of movable guarantee rights without transfer of possession. The first one is called 'movable mortgage', and it is foreseen for goods considered liable to an easier identification, almost similar to the one for immovable goods. The second one called 'pledge without transfer of possession' is foreseen, on the contrary, for goods or groups of goods with a less identifiable character.

In the movable mortgage, as occurs with the immovable mortgage, it is the publicity coming from the Registry that substitutes the one coming from possession. In the pledge without transfer of possession, the lack of possessory publicity is substituted due to the consideration that the pledge debtor, who keeps the possession of the pledged goods, can be made responsible in exactly the same way as a depositary of the goods. However, unlike a normal depositary, this pledge debtor may use the pledged goods if any detriment to their value is not produced (Article 59 LHMPDP).

334. The LHMPDP contains a number of general dispositions that reflect the common notes to both forms of security (Articles 1–11). For instance, these two rights must be purchased through a contract reflected in a notarial deed, and they must be registered in the former Registry of Movable Mortgage and Pledge without Transfer of Possession, currently called Registry of Movable Goods. However, the goods burdened with movable mortgage or pledge without transfer of possession

203. That is to say, the pledge right is degraded, with regard to the second obligation, to the *status* of a mere *ius retentionis*.

may not be alienated without the creditor's consent (Article 4 Law on Movable Mortgage and Pledge without Transfer of Possession). The mandatory sale in case the secured obligation is not fulfilled may be made either through judicial proceedings (Articles 681 et seq. LEC) or through notarial ones (Articles 86–91 and 94–95 LHMPDP).

335. Article 12 LHMPDP contains a *numerus clausus* of goods liable to movable mortgage: commercial establishments, motor vehicles, tramcars, railway carriages, airships, industrial machinery, intellectual property rights, and industrial property rights.[204] The contract must specify the maximum possible amount of description data to allow for their identification.

336. The catalogue of goods liable to pledge without transfer of possession is contained, also with the character of *numerus clausus*, in Articles 52–54 LHMPDP. Included are, on the one side, a number of goods related to agrarian and cattle exploitations (pending fruits and harvests, fruits or products already harvested, and animals together with their young). On the other side, goods of industrial or commercial nature are mentioned (machinery, merchandises, articles, and raw material in storage). Finally, the goods could also be burdened objects or collection of objects endowed with artistic or historical value (i.e., stamps, paintings, sculptures, porcelains, and books).

The Law 41/2007 has also introduced the pledge without transfer of possession upon credits, even future ones, in order to submit this specific real guarantee to the Register of Movable Goods' publicity. This is an important issue, especially in insolvency scenarios. There are some decisions by the TS on the subject of efficacy of a pledge on future credits when the pledge debtor becomes insolvent.[205] A recent reform of the Law on Insolvency (by Law 40/2015, of October 1) admits the efficacy of a pledge on future credits if it is stated in a notarial deed or, in absence of possession transfer, the pledge has been recorded in the Registry of Movable Goods.

Goods liable to movable mortgage may not be pledged without transfer of possession or that have already been mortgaged together with an estate. An ordinary pledge upon goods that have been burdened with pledge without possessory transfer may not be constituted (Article 55 LHMPDP).

§3. Retention Right, Compensation

I. Introduction

337. The study of two institutions that come indirectly in a sort of security for the holder of a credit will now be undertaken. Both of them have in common that they are based on the existence of a parallel relation of credit that links exactly the

204. Also commercial ships are liable to mortgage, but its regulation is contained in the Law of Naval Mortgage (21 Aug. 1893), which is still in force. This law creates the fiction of considering them as immovable goods, only for the purpose of mortgaging them.
205. *See* STS 22 Apr. 2008 and STS 6 Nov. 2013.

same subjects of a first-credit relation but in an inverse way; that is to say, the person that appears as creditor in the first relation fulfils the role of debtor in the second one and vice versa.

So, the fact of the creditor being a parallel debtor of his/her own debtor gives him/her an advantage that he/she would not have in the opposite case: By means of his/her own non-fulfilment, the creditor can either pressure the debtor to fulfil or counteract the effects of the latter's non-fulfilment.

II. Retention Right

338. The retention right can be defined as the power that the law grants a creditor for keeping himself/herself in possession of movable goods of his/her debtor, beyond the time when the goods should be returned, until the debtor pays a debt due. The delay in the return of the goods becomes a coercion mechanism to reach the fulfilment of the debtor's obligations. For instance, the CC provides a retention right: to the depositary for guaranteeing the payment of the amounts due because of the deposit (Article 1780 CC); to the mandatary in relation to the anticipated amounts or damages suffered because of the task developed (Article 1730 CC); to the person that effects a (reparation) work on a movable object of another person, for guaranteeing the payment of the price (Article 1600); to the usufructuary for certain expenses made because of the reparation of the usufructed object (Articles 522 and 502 CC); and in general to any possessor in good faith for the necessary expenses made in relation to the possessed object (Article 453 CC).

339. The retention right lies in the existence of a mutual relationship: Although a first subject is debtor of another person regarding the return of definite movable goods, the latter is at the same time debtor of the former regarding the payment of the expenses made in the goods or the damages suffered because of their possession.

This guarantee has been related to the *exceptio non adimpleti contractus*, because, as stated in the exception, an obligor (and obligee at the same time) denies the fulfilment of his/her duty because of the incomplete fulfilment of the obligation in charge of the obligee.

The retention right may also be related to the principle of good faith because it is contrary to this principle that an individual requires another to return goods without paying what the former owes to the latter.

340. It is important to underscore the different scope that the retention right has in comparison to the pledge, although the CC says, when referring to it, that the creditor vested in a retention right may retain goods 'as does a pledge creditor'.

Unlike the pledge, the retention right is circumscribed to a power of mere maintenance of the possession, without including any power to realize the value of the goods whose possession is retained.

III. Compensation

341. The compensation presupposes the existence of two people in such a manner that at the same time the first one is obligee with regard to the second and vice versa (Article 1195 CC). The effect of the compensation is extinguishing both obligations in the concurrent amount (Article 1202 CC).

From a practical point of view, the compensation finds its reason for being in the convenience of simplifying the fulfilment of the obligations, substituting two payments with effective transference of funds by a simple arithmetic operation.

The compensation is also explained as necessary to avoid the objectively disloyal character of the behaviour consisting of a request of payment of a debt when at the same time the person who requests it is obligor in relation to the other person.

In addition, the compensation becomes a privileged way of liquidating a debt, which doubtlessly approximates it to a security. The creditor that has the power to set off enjoys a powerful reinforcement of his/her credit because he/she does not actually need to wait until the debtor pays the debt to obtain the satisfaction of his/her credit. Understandably, this effect means a special advantage for the creditor who may obtain compensation when he/she concurs with other creditors of his/her debtor in an insolvency process.

342. According to Article 1196 CC, it is necessary that the following requirements are fulfilled in order for the compensation to operate: (a) the two debts are homogeneous from a qualitative point of view (monetary debts and debts of fungible goods of the same species and quality); (b) both debts are already due, and they are payable and defined in cash, which excludes compensation for debts submitted to a term or condition; (c) each obligor appears as the principal responsible of the debt; and (d) the debts are not under judicial controversy, promoted by a third party. Moreover, set-off may be made neither in relation to the obligation of return imposed to depositaries and borrowers nor be opposed by the debtor for a legal obligation of alimony (Article 1200 CC).

§4. Direct Claim

343. In some cases, the law allows the creditor to bring an action *proprio nomine* against a third party – debtor of his/her debtor – to claim him/her the satisfaction of the former credit. Therefore in the direct action, the creditor does not occupy the position of his/her debtor, but he/she may act in his/her own name against a person that has a debt with his/her debtor.

It is obvious that the direct claim amplifies the credit's efficacy beyond the *inter partes* sphere. Furthermore, in case of concurrence with other creditors of the (first) debtor, the creditor empowered with a direct claim has the possibility of taking out an action from the debtor's patrimony (his credit against a third person) and at the same time satisfying with priority his/her credit.

344. Some cases of direct claim foreseen in the legal order of Spain would be the case that the mandator may bring against the substitute of the mandatary (Article

1722 CC); the case that the lessor may bring against the sub-lessee of the leased goods (Article 1552 CC); or the case that the victim of an accident may bring against the insurance company that assured the risk (Article 76 of the Law on the Contract of Insurance).

Selected Bibliography

§1. Books

I. General Works

Albaladejo García, M. *Derecho Civil, III* (*Derecho de bienes*). Barcelona: J.Mª Bosch, 2004.

Albaladejo García, M. & S. Díaz Alabart (eds.). *Comentarios al Código Civil y Compilaciones Forales* (many volumes). Madrid: Edersa, different years.

Álvarez Caperochipi, J.A. Curso de Derecho Civil. Tomo I. *Curso de Derechos reales*. Volumen I. Propiedad y Derechos Reales. Granada: Comares, 2005.

Álvarez Caperochipi, J.A. *Derecho inmobiliario registral*. Granada: Comares, 2006.

Bercovitz Rodríguez-Cano, R. (ed.). *Comentarios al Código Civil*. 4th ed. Cizur Menor (Navarra): Aranzadi-Thomson Reuters, 2013.

Bercovitz Rodríguez-Cano, R. (ed.). *Comentarios a la Ley de Propiedad Intelectual*. 4th ed. Madrid: Tecnos, 2017.

Bercovitz Rodríguez-Cano, R. (ed.). *Comentarios a la Ley de Propiedad Horizontal*. 4th ed. Cizur Menor (Navarra): Aranzadi, 2010.

Bercovitz Rodríguez-Cano, R. (ed.). *Comentarios al Convenio de Berna para la protección de las obras literarias y artísticas*. Madrid: Tecnos, 2013.

Bercovitz, R., et al. (eds.). *Comentario del Código Civil. I and II*. Madrid: Ministerio de Justicia, 1993.

Bercovitz Rodríguez-Cano, R. (ed.). *Manual de Derecho Civil. Derechos Reales*. 5th ed. Madrid: Bercal, 2015.

Bercovitz Rodríguez-Cano, R. (ed.). *Tratado de contratos*. Valencia: Tirant lo Blanch, 2009, 2013.

Castán Tobeñas, J. *Derecho civil español, común y foral*. II. Madrid: Reus, 1992.

De los Mozos, J.L. *Estudios sobre Derecho de los bienes*. Madrid: Montecorvo, 1991.

Díez-Picazo, L. *Fundamentos del Derecho Civil Patrimonial*. III. 5th ed. Madrid: Cívitas, 2008.

Díez-Picazo, L. & A. Gullón. *Sistema de Derecho civil*. III. Madrid: Tecnos, 1998, 2001, 2012.

García García, J.M. *Derecho Inmobiliario Registral o Hipotecario. I and II*. Madrid: Cívitas, 1988 and 1993.

Lacruz Berdejo, J.L., et al. *Elementos de Derecho Civil. III* (3 vols). Madrid: Dykinson, 2003/2009.

Merryman, J.H. *The Civil Law Tradition*. 3rd ed. Stanford, CA: Stanford University Press, 2007.

Peña Bernaldo de Quirós, M. *Derechos reales. Derecho hipotecario. I and II*. 3rd ed. Madrid: Centro de Estudios Registrales, 2001.

Roca Sastre, R. & L. Roca-Sastre Muncunill. *Derecho hipotecario*. Several volumes. Barcelona: Bosch, different years.

Vallet de Goytisolo, J. *Estudios sobre Derecho de Cosas*. Madrid: Montecorvo, 1986.

II. Monographs

Abella Rubio, J.M. *La división de la cosa común en el Código Civil*. Madrid: Dykinson, 2005.

Alas, L., D. De Buen & E. Ramos. *De la usucapión*. Madrid: Centro de Estudios Históricos, 1916.

Arespacochaga, J. *El trust, la fiducia y figuras afines*. Madrid-Barcelona: Marcial Pons, 2000.

Arechederra Aranzadi, L.I. *Propiedad y constitución de servidumbres*. Madrid: Dykinson, 1993.

Ballarín Hernández, R. *La hipoteca*. Madrid: Montecorvo, 1980.

Beltrán de Heredia y Castaño, J. *La comunidad de bienes en Derecho español*. Madrid: Revista de Derecho Privado, 1954.

Beltrán de Heredia y Onís, P. *El derecho de retención en el Código civil español*. Salamanca: Universidad de Salamanca, 1955.

Bercovitz Álvarez, G. *Tradición instrumental y posesión*. Pamplona: Aranzadi, 1999.

Blasco Gascó, F. de P. *La hipoteca inmobiliaria y el crédito hipotecario*. Valencia: Tirant lo blanch, 2000.

Carrasco Perera, A. *'Ius aedificandi' y accesión*. Madrid: Montecorvo, 1986.

Carrasco Perera, A. *Relaciones civiles con contenido urbanístico*. Pamplona: Aranzadi, 1999.

Carrasco Perera, A., et al. *Derecho de la construcción y la vivienda*. 7th ed. Madrid: Dilex, 2012.

Carrasco Perera, A. (ed.). *Tratado de garantías*. 2nd ed. Cizur Menor (Navarra): Aranzadi-Thomson, 2008.

Checa Martínez, M. *El trust angloamericano en el Derecho español*. Madrid: Mc Graw Hill, 1998.

De la Cámara Álvarez, M. *La adquisición 'a non domino' de bienes muebles*. Madrid: Editoriales de Derecho Reunidas, 1982.

De la Iglesia Monje, I. *El derecho de superficie, aspectos civiles y registrales*. Madrid: Centro de Estudios Registrales, 1996.

De los Mozos, J.L. *El derecho de propiedad. Crisis y retorno a la tradición jurídica*. Madrid: Editoriales de Derecho Reunidas, 1993.

De los Mozos, J.L. *El derecho de superficie en general y su relación con la planificación urbanística*. Madrid: Ministerio de la Vivienda, 1974.

De los Mozos, J.L. *Estudios de Derecho agrario*. Valladolid: Universidad de Valladolid, 1981.

Del Arco Torres, M.A. & M. Pons González. *Régimen jurídico de las servidumbres*. Granada: Comares, 1994.

Díez-Picazo, L., et al. *Propiedad y Derecho Civil*. Madrid: Colegio de Registradores de la Propiedad y Mercantiles de España, 2006.

Durán Rivacoba, R. *La propiedad en garantía. Prohibición del pacto comisorio*. Pamplona: Aranzadi, 1998.

Feliú Rey, M.I. *La prohibición del pacto comisorio y la opción en garantía*. Madrid: Cívitas, 1995.

Fernández Domingo, J.I. *Los derechos reales de uso y habitación*. Madrid: Dykinson, 1994.

Fuenteseca, C. *El negocio fiduciario en la jurisprudencia del Tribunal Supremo*. Barcelona: José Mª Bosch, 1997.

Fuenteseca, C. *La posesión mediata e inmediata*. Madrid: Dykinson, 2002.

Garrido, J.M. *Garantías reales, privilegios y par condicio*. Madrid: Centro de Estudios Registrales, 1999.

Guilarte Gutiérrez, V. *La constitución voluntaria de servidumbres en el Derecho español*. Madrid: Montecorvo, 1984.

Hernández Gil, A. *La posesión*. Madrid: Cívitas, 1980.

Hernández Gil, A. *Las relaciones de vecindad en el Código civil*. Madrid: Real Academia de Jurisprudencia y Legislación, 1985.

Lete del Río, J.M. *Protección del derecho de propiedad*. Santiago de Compostela: Universidad de Santiago de Compostela, 1975.

López y López, A. *La disciplina constitucional de la propiedad privada*. Madrid: Tecnos, 1988.

Martínez-Gijón Machuca, P. *Los registros mercantil y de bienes muebles*. Tomo 2: El registro de bienes muebles. Madrid: Marcial Pons, 2006.

Miquel González, J.Mª. *La posesión de bienes muebles*. Madrid: Montecorvo, 1979.

Moralejo Imbernón, N. *El contrato de hipoteca inmobiliaria*. Cizur Menor: Aranzadi Thomson Reuters 2010.

Montés Penadés, V.L. *La propiedad privada en el sistema del Derecho civil contemporáneo*. Madrid: Cívitas, 1980.

Rebolledo Varela, A.L. *Tratado de servidumbres*. 2nd ed. Cizur Menor (Navarra): Aranzadi-Thomson, 2007.

Rojo Ajuria, L. *La compensación como garantía*. Madrid: Cívitas, 1992.

Vallet, de Goytisolo. *Estudios sobre garantías reales*. Madrid: Montecorvo, 1973.

§2. Articles and Notes

Albaladejo García, M. 'Concepto, estructura y clases de posesión'. *Revista de Derecho Privado* (1962): 588.

Alonso Pérez, M. 'Las relaciones de vecindad'. *Anuario de Derecho Civil* (1983): 357.

Álvarez Caperochipi, J.A. 'La posesión y el Registro de la Propiedad'. *Revista de Derecho Privado* (1978): 465.

Arroyo i Amayuelas, E. 'Los patrimonios fiduciarios y el "trust"'. *Revista Crítica de Derecho Inmobiliario*. No. 693 (2006): 11.

Cámara Lapuente, S. 'Operaciones fiduciarias o trusts en Derecho español'. *Revista Crítica de Derecho Inmobiliario*, No. 654 (September–October 1999): 1757.

Selected Bibliography

Camy Sánchez-Cañete, B. 'Comentarios a la Ley de Hipoteca Mobiliaria'. *Revista Crítica de Derecho Inmobiliario*, Nos 336–337, 338–339, 340–341 (May–June, July–August, September–October 1956): 347, 508, 654 (three parts).

Castellanos Ruiz, E. 'El "trust" en el Derecho sucesorio español'. *Revista Crítica de Derecho Inmobiliario*, No. 704 (2007): 2429.

Clavería Gosálbez, L.H. 'Notas sobre el denominado negocio jurídico fiduciario'. *Revista General de Legislación y Jurisprudencia* (2012): 541.

Cerdeira Bravo de Mansilla, G. 'La accesión invertida: su génesis y evolución en la jurisprudencia'. *Revista Aranzadi de Derecho Patrimonial*, No. 23 (2009): 25.

Cobacho Gómez, J.A. 'Reflexiones sobre el derecho de superficie urbana'. *Revista Crítica de Derecho Inmobiliario*, No. 710 (2008): 2281.

Costas Rodal, L. 'La multipropiedad en España: valoración de la Ley 42/1998 sobre Derechos de Aprovechamiento por Turno de Bienes Inmuebles de Uso Turístico'. *Actualidad Civil*, No. 44 (2000): 1585.

De la Cuesta Sáenz, J.M. 'El estatuto jurídico del suelo con destino agrario'. *Derecho Privado y Constitución*, No. 3 (1994): 131.

Díez-Picazo, L. 'Autonomía y derechos reales'. *Revista Crítica de Derecho Inmobiliario*, No. 463 (November–December 1976): 273.

Díez-Picazo, L. 'La modificación de las relaciones jurídico-reales y la teoría de la accesión'. *Revista Crítica de Derecho Inmobiliario*, No. 455 (July–August 1966): 829.

Font Boix, V. 'La adquisición registral "a non domino"'. *Revista Crítica de Derecho Inmobiliario*, No. 463 (November–December 1967): 1607.

García García, J.M. 'La finca como base del sistema inmobiliario'. *Revista Crítica de Derecho Inmobiliario*, No. 625 (November–December 1994): 2437.

García García, J.M. 'La función registral y la seguridad del tráfico inmobiliario'. *Revista Crítica de Derecho Inmobiliario*, No. 625 (November–December 1994): 2239.

Gordillo Cañas, A. 'Bases del derecho de cosas y principios inmobiliarios registrales: sistema español'. *Anuario de Derecho Civil* (1995): 527.

Jordano Fraga, F. 'Prenda regular, prenda irregular y prenda de crédito'. *Anuario de Derecho Civil* (1990): 305.

Lalaguna Domínguez, E. 'Los modos de adquirir la propiedad y los contratos de finalidad traslativa en el Derecho español'. *Revista de Derecho Privado* (1973): 383.

Mastroprieto, B. 'Acto de destinación y "trust": dos modelos a confrontar'. *Revista General de Legislación y Jurisprudencia* (2012): 551.

Mateo y Villa, I. 'De la fiducia gestión'. *Revista Crítica de Derecho Inmobiliario*, No. 704 (2007): 2585.

Miquel González, J.Mª. 'Notas sobre el artículo 464 del Código civil y la reciente jurisprudencia'. *Anuario de Derecho Civil* (1999): 565.

Morales Moreno, A.M. 'La inscripción y el justo título de usucapión'. *Anuario de Derecho Civil* (1971): 1123.

Moreno Quesada, B. 'La protección del crédito en las garantías reales mobiliarias'. *Revista de Derecho Privado* (1997): 251.

Pau Pedrón, A. 'Efectos de la inscripción en la constitución de los derechos reales'. *Revista Crítica de Derecho Inmobiliario*, No. 625 (November–December 1994): 2187.

Pardo Núñez, C. 'Confusión de patrimonios y publicidad registral: el caso del "trust"'. *Revista Crítica de Derecho Inmobiliario*, No. 697 (2006): 1909.

Roca Sastre, R.Mª. 'El problema de la relación que respecto del artículo 34 L.H. guarda el articulo 32'. *Revista Crítica de Derecho Inmobiliario* (1965): 781.

Rojo Ajuria, L. 'Las garantías mobiliarias'. *Anuario de Derecho Civil* (1989): 717.

Sánchez Aristi, R. 'La adquisición por Ley de la propiedad y los demás derechos reales sobre los bienes'. *Aranzadi Civil* No. 19 (February 2001): 13.

§3. General Case Law Surveys

For searching sentences of the TS, probably the most common source among Spanish scholars, lawyers, and courts continues to be the Aranzadi compilation of jurisprudence. Citations are written in brackets, after the abbreviation for the name of the court and the date of the sentence, the abbreviation for the compilation, followed by the year and the reference number assigned to the sentence. For example, a sentence rendered by the TS on 27 March 1995 is quoted as 'STS 27 March 1995 (Aranzadi Compilation of Jurisprudence (RJA) 1995, 2325)'. The Aranzadi compilation of jurisprudence (currently Aranzadi-Westlaw) has been converted into an electronic database, available either offline or online (*see* <www.aranzadi.es> and <www.westlaw.es>). Other well-known electronic databases of jurisprudence are *El Derecho* and *La Ley* (*see* respectively <www.elderecho.com> and <www.laley.net>). Obviously, the reference numbers assigned by every one of these compilations are different. A free official database of jurisprudence is also available through the official web site of the General Council for the Judiciary, <www.poderjudicial.es/search/index.jsp>.

Furthermore, Aranzadi has published a specific compilation of sentences (not only rendered by the TS) exclusively referring to the field of Civil Law. It is titled *Aranzadi Civil* and it also contains studies on the matter. A repertoire of the most significant sentences rendered by the TS in Civil Law, organized by subject and with comments by reputed scholars, has been published by a four-month review since 1983. This review, edited by Prof. Dr R. Bercovitz, is titled *Cuadernos Cívitas de Jurisprudencia Civil* (Civitas Bulletin of Civil Jurisprudence).

The jurisprudence of the TC is also available through all the electronic databases mentioned above, as well as through the official Web site of the TC (*see* <www.tribunalconstitucional.es/es/jurisprudencia/Paginas/Buscador.aspx>). The reference numbers for the sentences of the TC, which are always quoted together with the date of the sentence, are officially assigned and therefore do not vary in the different compilations (e.g., STC 37/1987, 26 March 1987).

Selected Bibliography

Index

The numbers here refer to paragraph numbers.

Index

www.ingramcontent.com/pod-product-compliance
Lightning Source LLC
Chambersburg PA
CBHW071342230926
51846CB00002B/425
* 9 7 8 9 4 0 3 5 1 3 4 4 7 *